INVENTIONS AND DISCOVERY

CHARLES DARWIN
AND THE THEORY OF EVOLUTION

by Heather Adamson

illustrated by Gordon Purcell and
Al Milgrom

Consultant:
Noah K. Whiteman, PhD
Postdoctoral Fellow
Harvard University
Museum of Comparative Zoology
Cambridge, Massachusetts

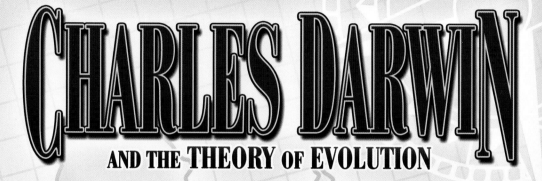

Capstone
press

Mankato, Minnesota

Graphic Library is published by Capstone Press,
151 Good Counsel Drive, P.O. Box 669, Mankato, Minnesota 56002.
www.capstonepress.com

Printed in the United States of America

1 2 3 4 5 6 12 11 10 09 08 07

Library of Congress Cataloging-in-Publication Data
Adamson, Heather, 1974–
Charles Darwin and the theory of evolution / by Heather Adamson; illustrated by Gordon Purcell and Al Milgrom.
p. cm. —(Graphic library. Inventions and discovery)
Summary: "In graphic novel format, tells the story of how Charles Darwin developed his controversial theory of evolution based on the research he conducted during his voyage on the HMS Beagle"—Provided by publisher.
Includes bibliographical references and index.
ISBN-13: 978-1-4296-0145-0 (hardcover)
ISBN-10: 1-4296-0145-0 (hardcover)
1. Darwin, Charles, 1809–1882. 2. Naturalists—England—Biography—Juvenile literature. 3. Evolution (Biology)—Juvenile literature. I. Purcell, Gordon. II. Milgrom, Al. III. Title. IV. Series.
QH31.D2A75 2008
576.8'2092—dc22
[B] 2007005659

Designers
Thomas Emery and Kim Brown

Colorist
Krista Ward

Editor
Christine Peterson

Editor's note: Direct quotations from primary sources are indicated by a yellow background.

Direct quotations appear on the following pages:
Page 7, quote from a letter by Darwin, as published in *The Life and Letters of Charles Darwin*, edited by Francis Darwin (New York: D. Appleton & Co., 1901).
Page 16, from a September 17, 1835, entry in Darwin's *Beagle* diary (http://www.aboutdarwin.com/voyage/voyage08.html).

TABLE OF CONTENTS

CHAPTER 1 ALWAYS A NATURALIST

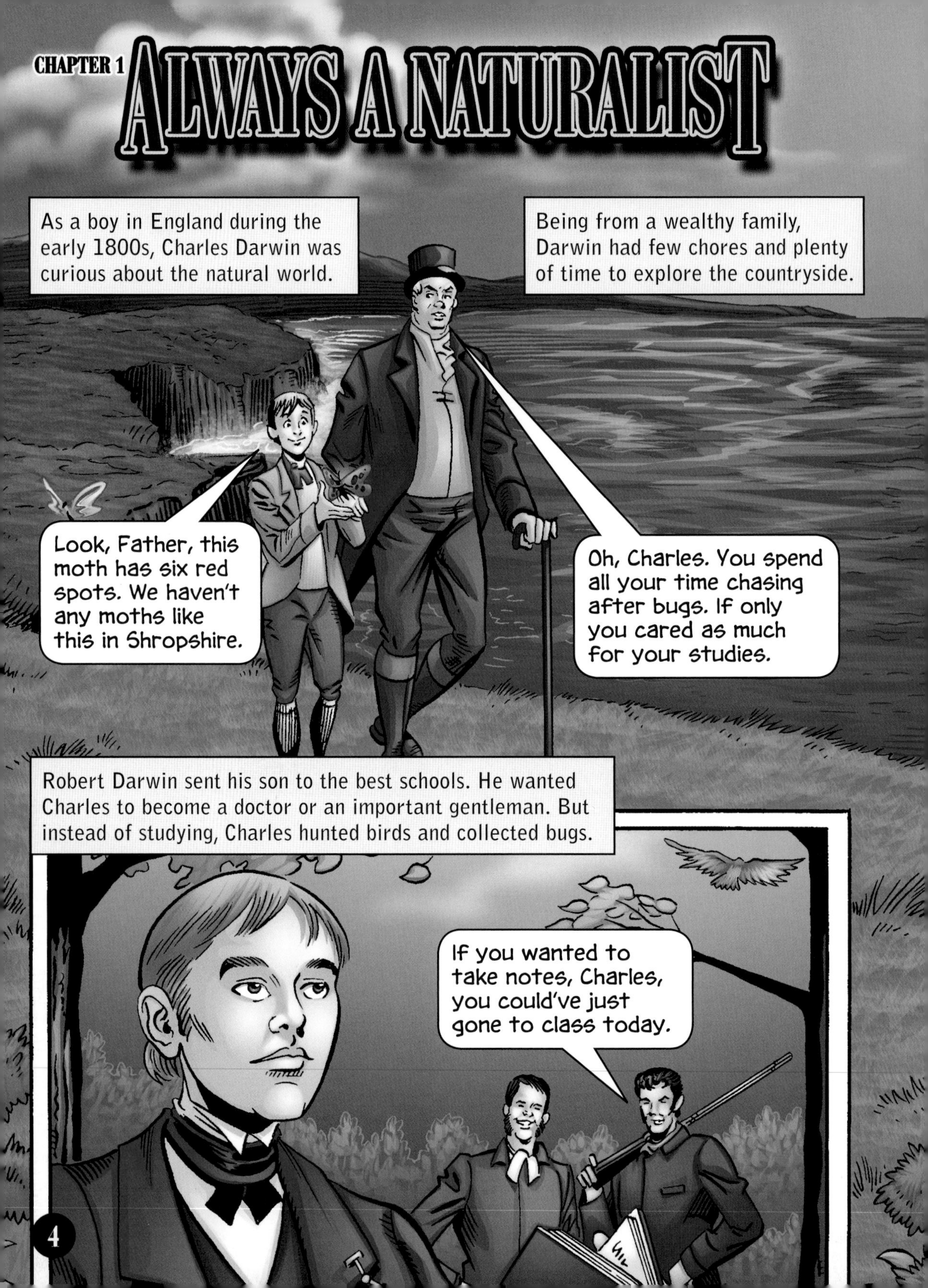
As a boy in England during the early 1800s, Charles Darwin was curious about the natural world.
Being from a wealthy family, Darwin had few chores and plenty of time to explore the countryside.
Look, Father, this moth has six red spots. We haven't any moths like this in Shropshire.
Oh, Charles. You spend all your time chasing after bugs. If only you cared as much for your studies.
Robert Darwin sent his son to the best schools. He wanted Charles to become a doctor or an important gentleman. But instead of studying, Charles hunted birds and collected bugs.
If you wanted to take notes, Charles, you could've just gone to class today.

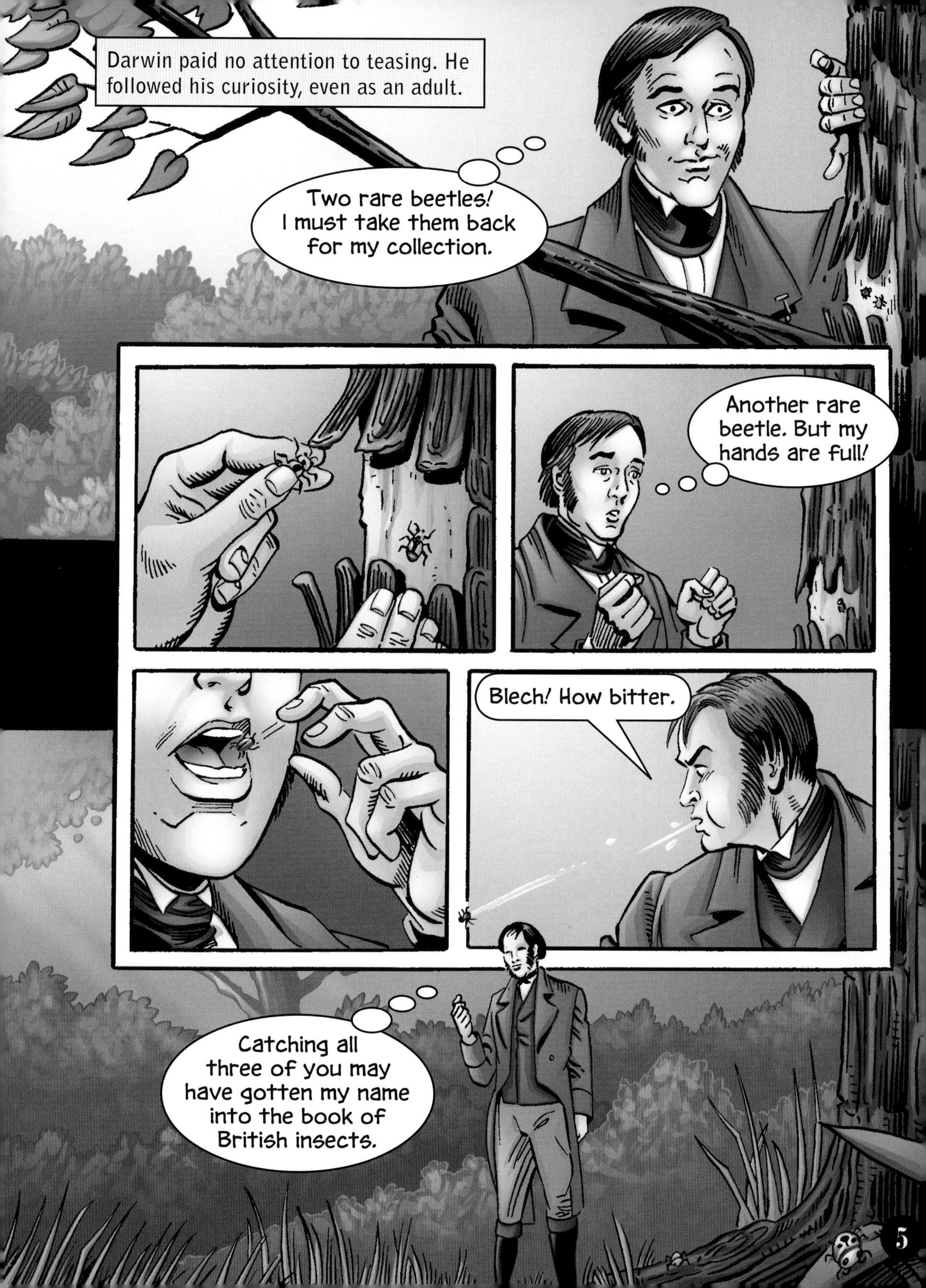
Darwin paid no attention to teasing. He followed his curiosity, even as an adult.
Two rare beetles! I must take them back for my collection.
Another rare beetle. But my hands are full!
Blech! How bitter.
Catching all three of you may have gotten my name into the book of British insects.

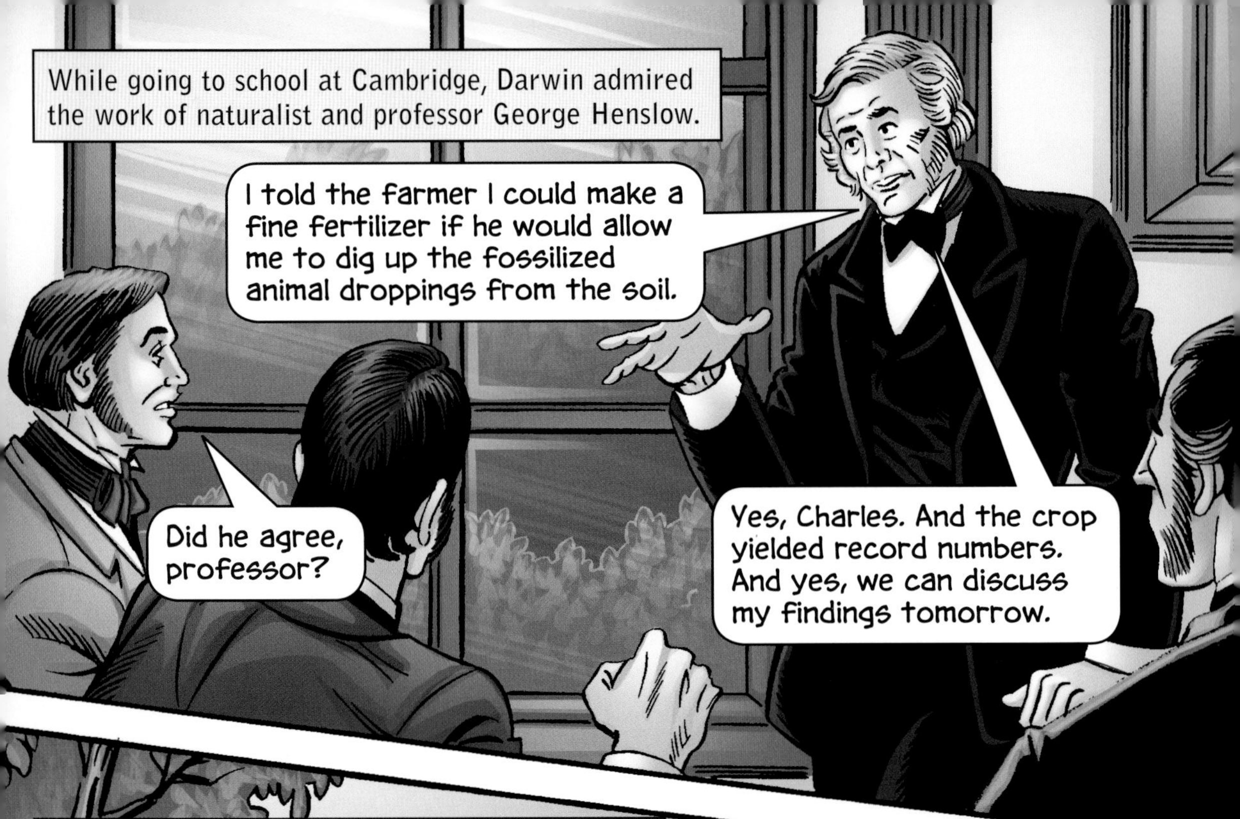
While going to school at Cambridge, Darwin admired the work of naturalist and professor George Henslow.
I told the farmer I could make a fine fertilizer if he would allow me to dig up the fossilized animal droppings from the soil.
Did he agree, professor?
Yes, Charles. And the crop yielded record numbers. And yes, we can discuss my findings tomorrow.

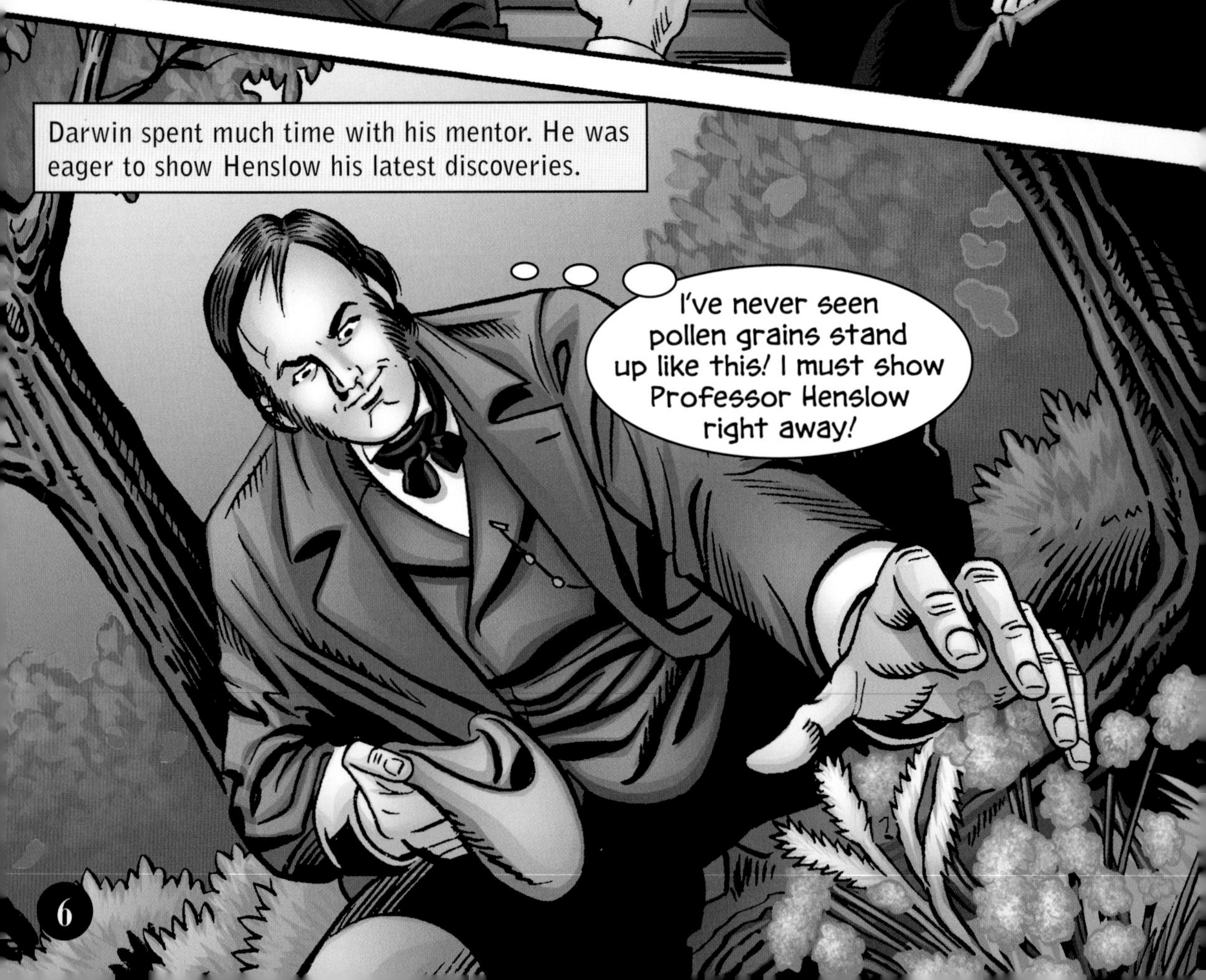
Darwin spent much time with his mentor. He was eager to show Henslow his latest discoveries.
I've never seen pollen grains stand up like this! I must show Professor Henslow right away!

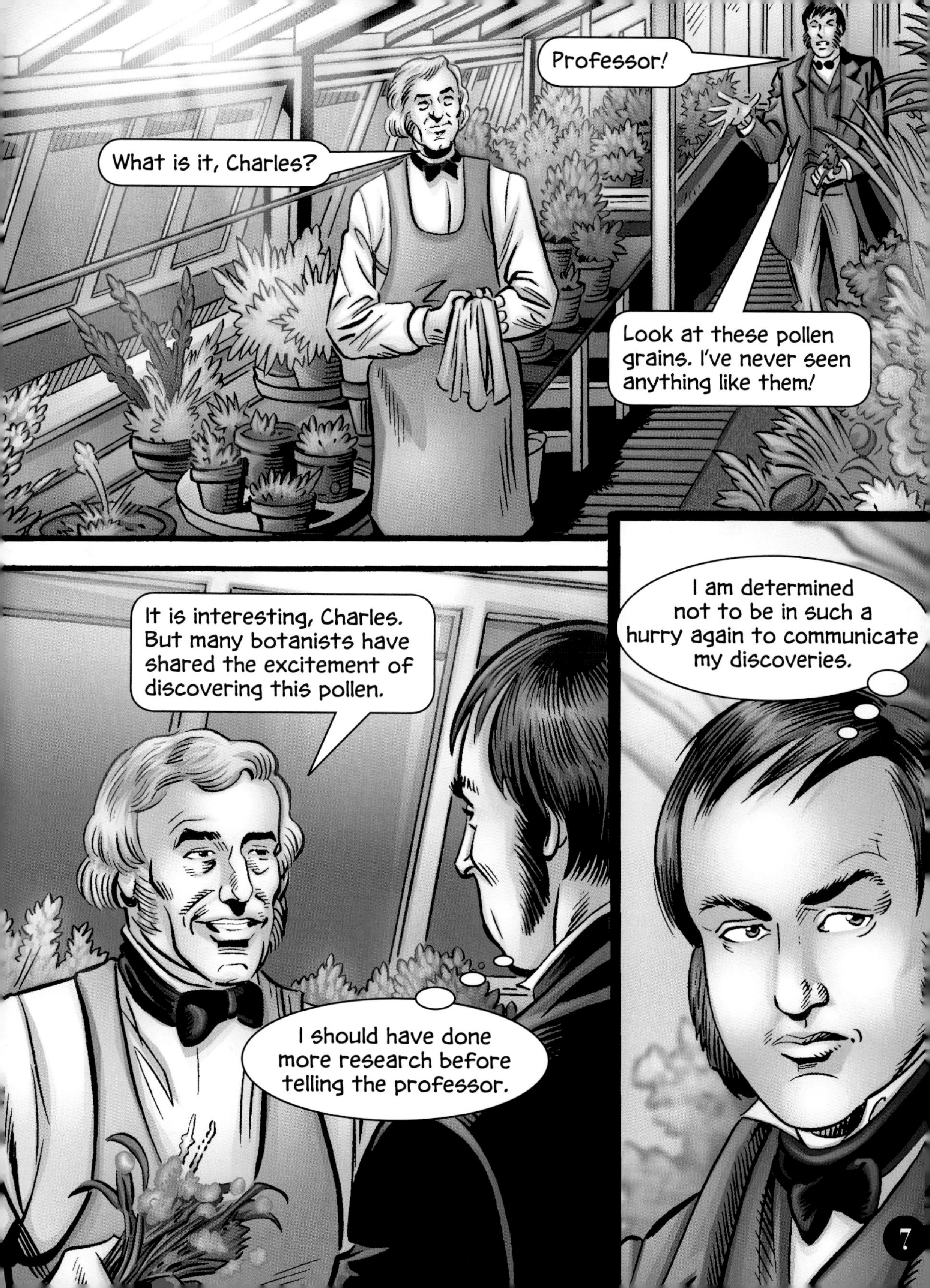
Professor!
What is it, Charles?
Look at these pollen grains. I've never seen anything like them!
It is interesting, Charles. But many botanists have shared the excitement of discovering this pollen.
I should have done more research before telling the professor.
I am determined not to be in such a hurry again to communicate my discoveries.

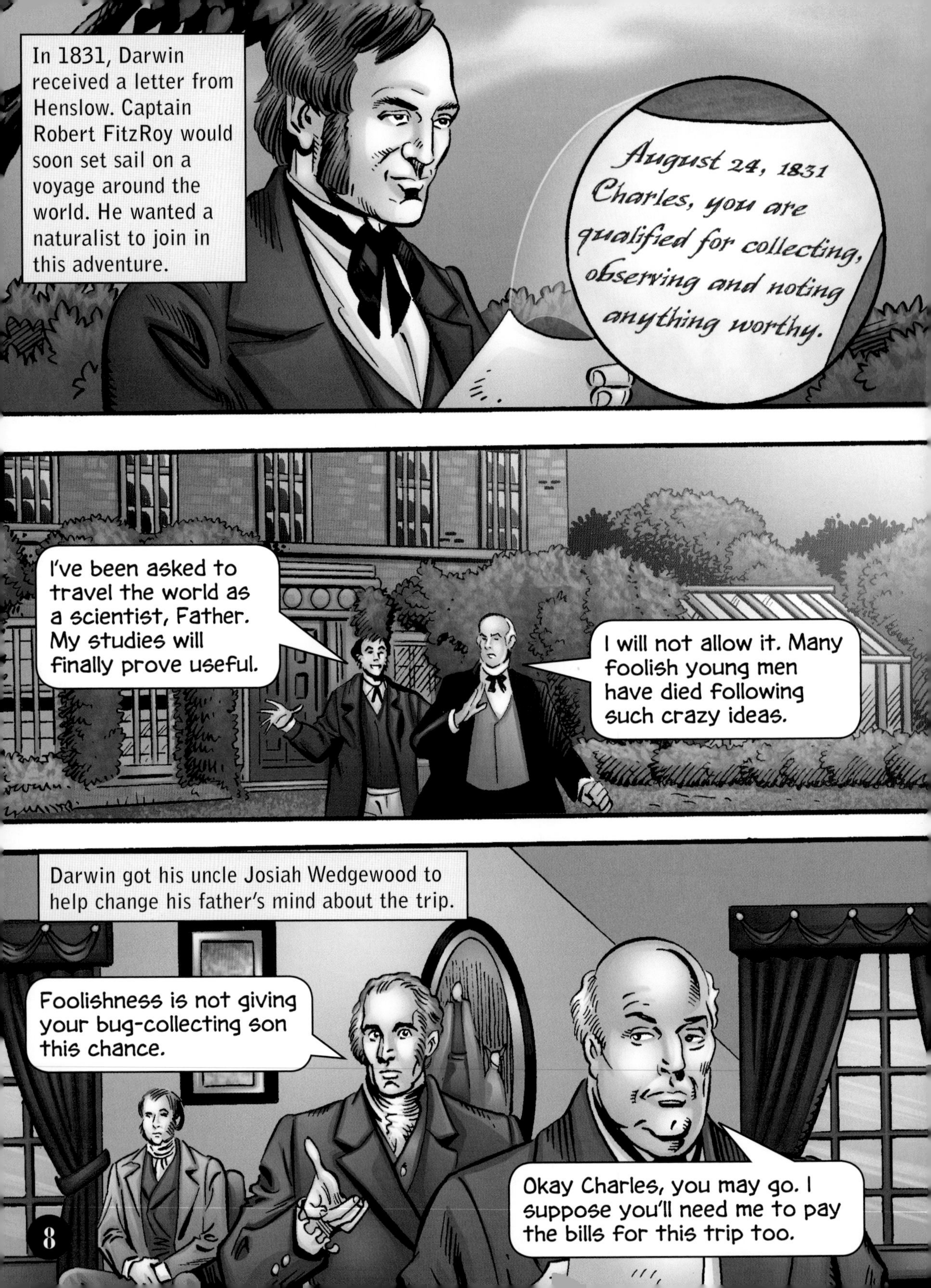
In 1831, Darwin received a letter from Henslow. Captain Robert FitzRoy would soon set sail on a voyage around the world. He wanted a naturalist to join in this adventure.
August 24, 1831
Charles, you are qualified for collecting, observing and noting anything worthy.
I've been asked to travel the world as a scientist, Father. My studies will finally prove useful.
I will not allow it. Many foolish young men have died following such crazy ideas.
Darwin got his uncle Josiah Wedgewood to help change his father's mind about the trip.
Foolishness is not giving your bug-collecting son this chance.
Okay Charles, you may go. I suppose you'll need me to pay the bills for this trip too.

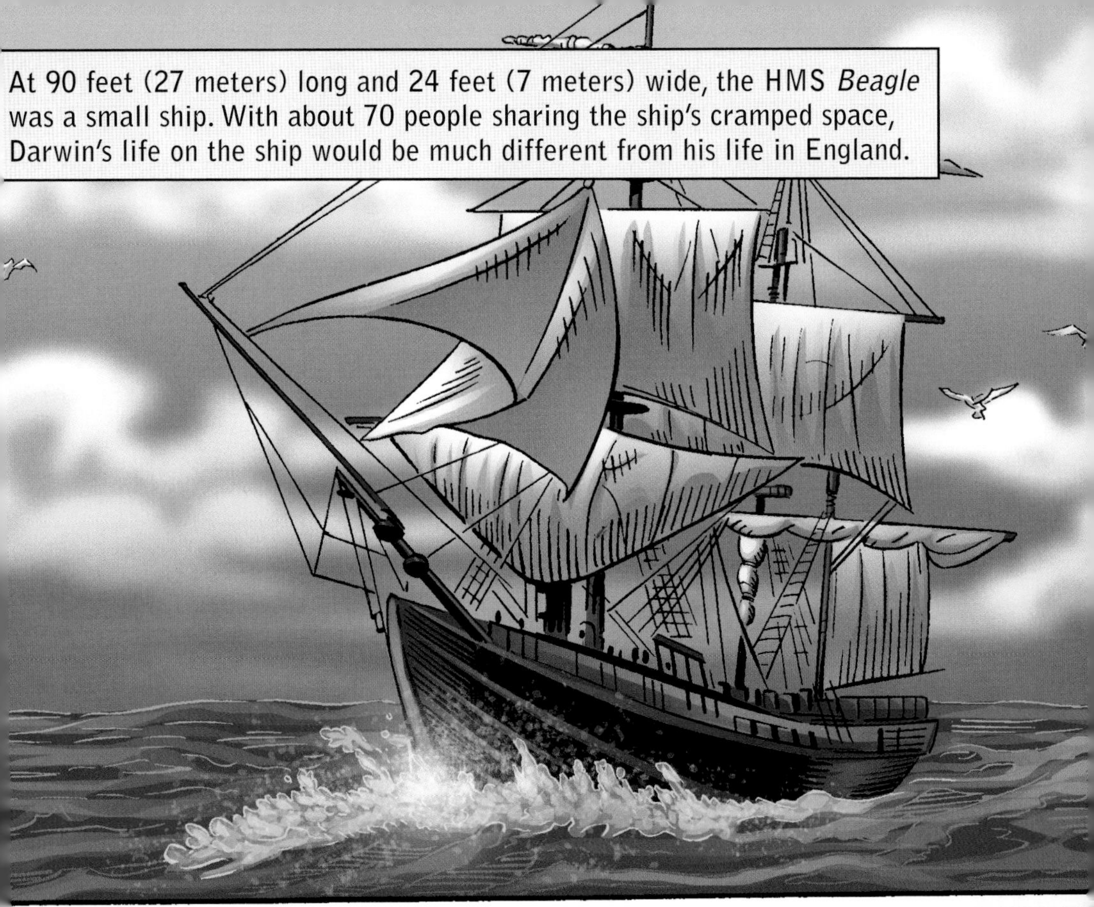
At 90 feet (27 meters) long and 24 feet (7 meters) wide, the HMS *Beagle* was a small ship. With about 70 people sharing the ship's cramped space, Darwin's life on the ship would be much different from his life in England.

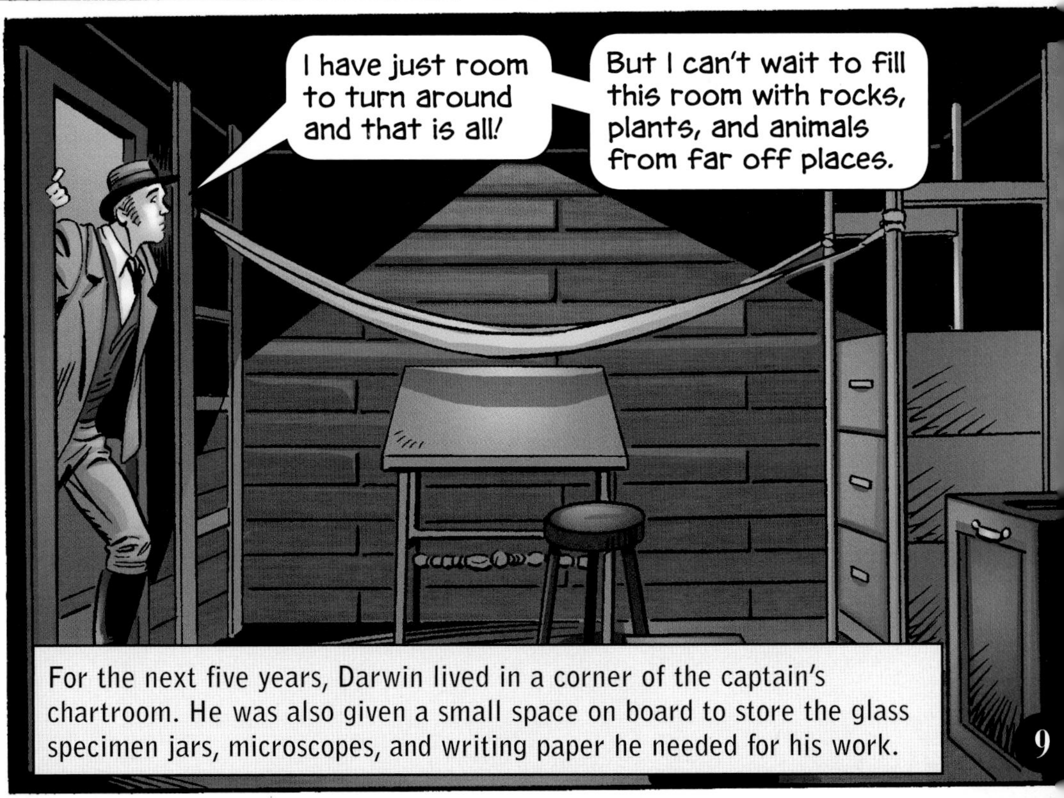
I have just room to turn around and that is all!
But I can't wait to fill this room with rocks, plants, and animals from far off places.
For the next five years, Darwin lived in a corner of the captain's chartroom. He was also given a small space on board to store the glass specimen jars, microscopes, and writing paper he needed for his work.

CHAPTER 2 VOYAGE OF THE HMS BEAGLE

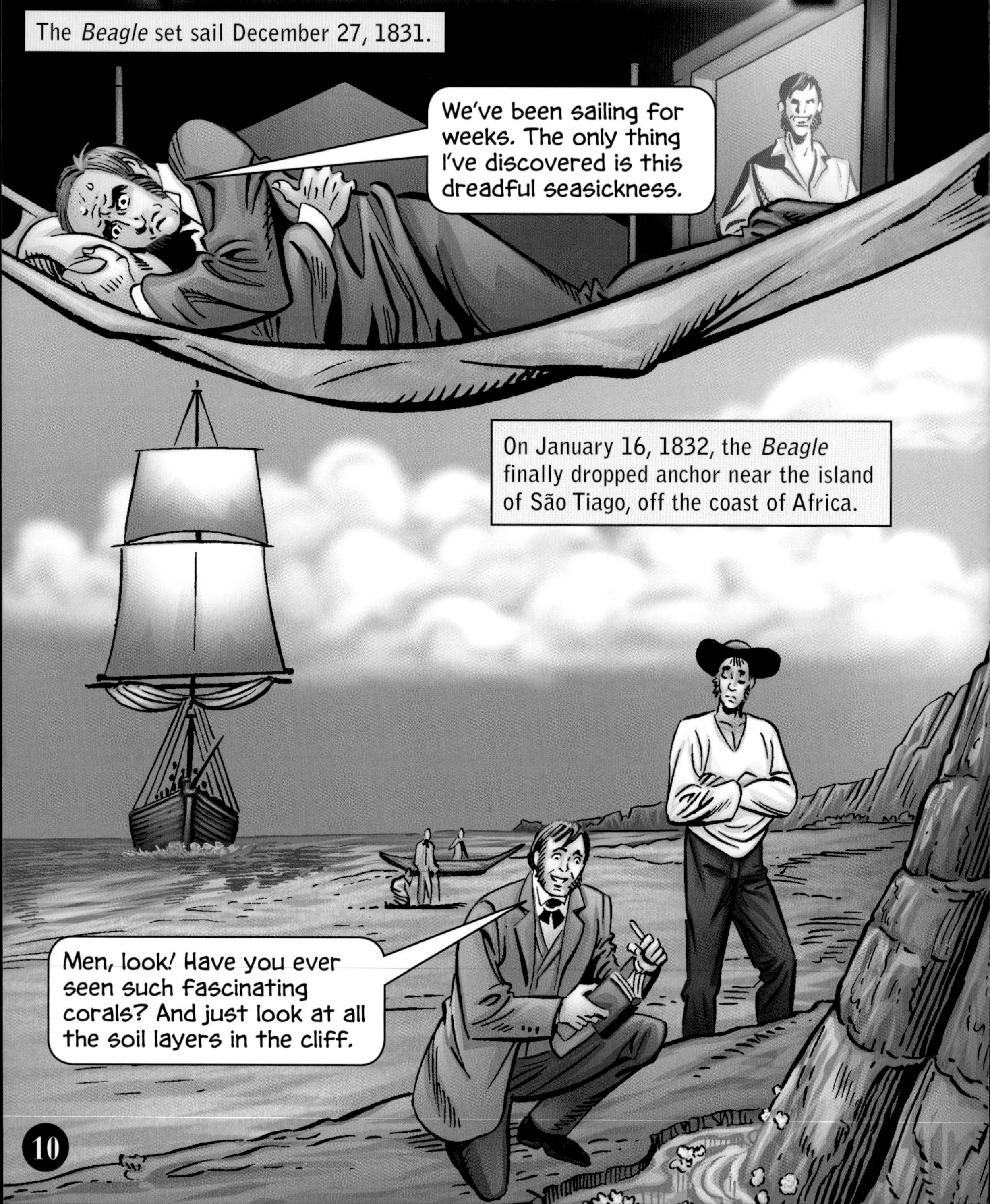
The *Beagle* set sail December 27, 1831.
We've been sailing for weeks. The only thing I've discovered is this dreadful seasickness.
On January 16, 1832, the *Beagle* finally dropped anchor near the island of São Tiago, off the coast of Africa.
Men, look! Have you ever seen such fascinating corals? And just look at all the soil layers in the cliff.

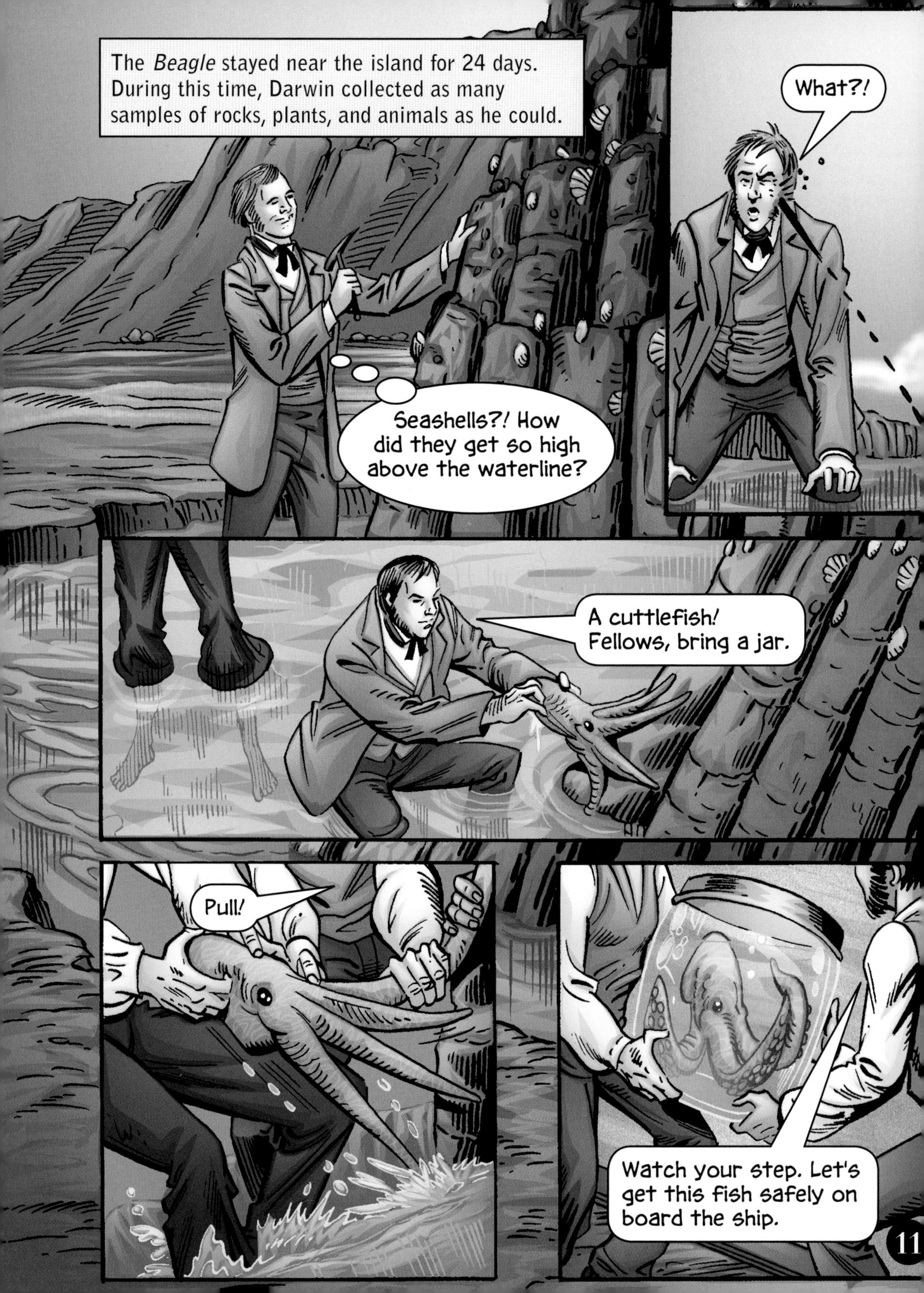
The *Beagle* stayed near the island for 24 days. During this time, Darwin collected as many samples of rocks, plants, and animals as he could.
Seashells?! How did they get so high above the waterline?
What?!
A cuttlefish! Fellows, bring a jar.
Pull!
Watch your step. Let's get this fish safely on board the ship.

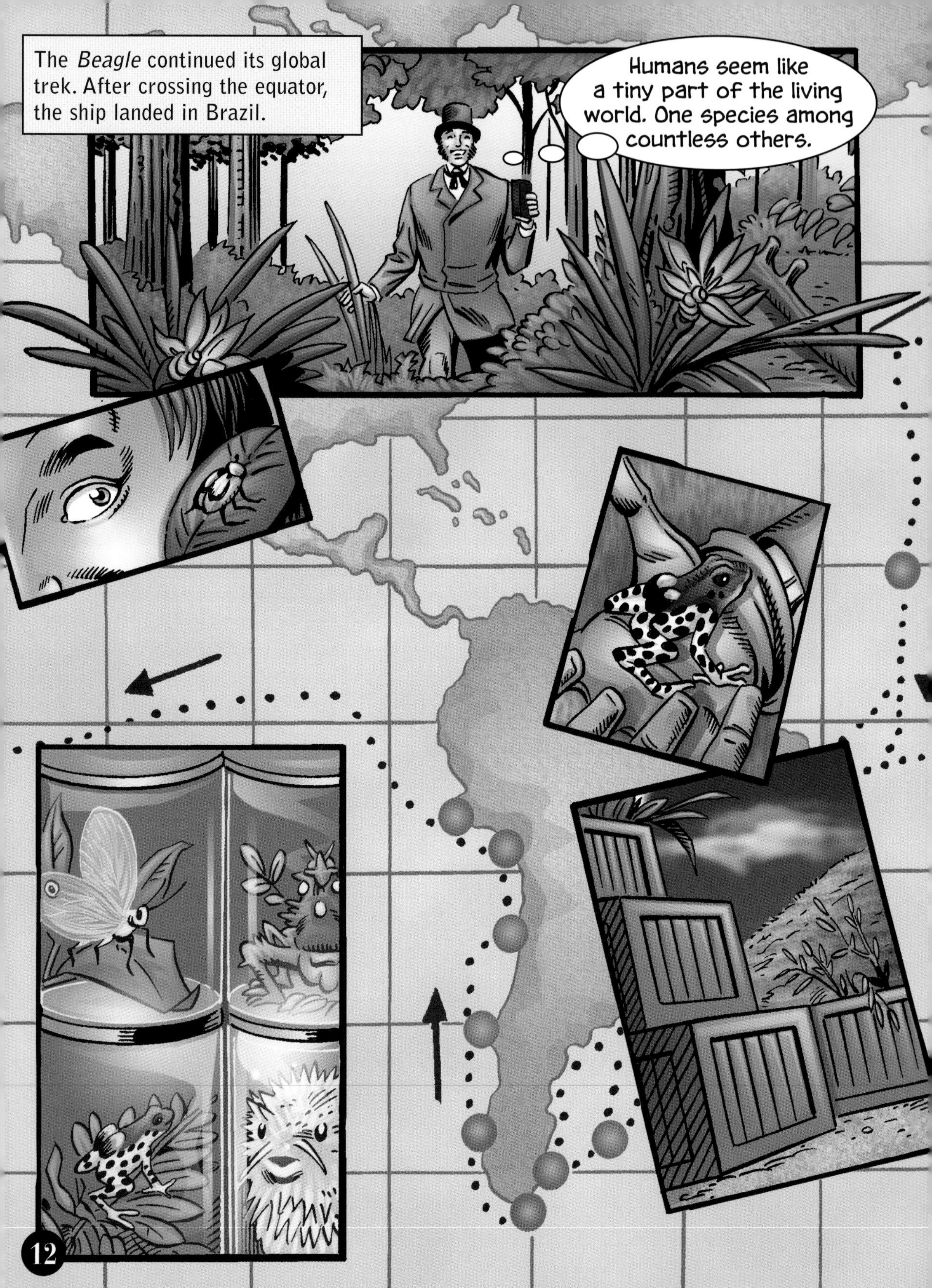
The *Beagle* continued its global trek. After crossing the equator, the ship landed in Brazil.
Humans seem like a tiny part of the living world. One species among countless others.

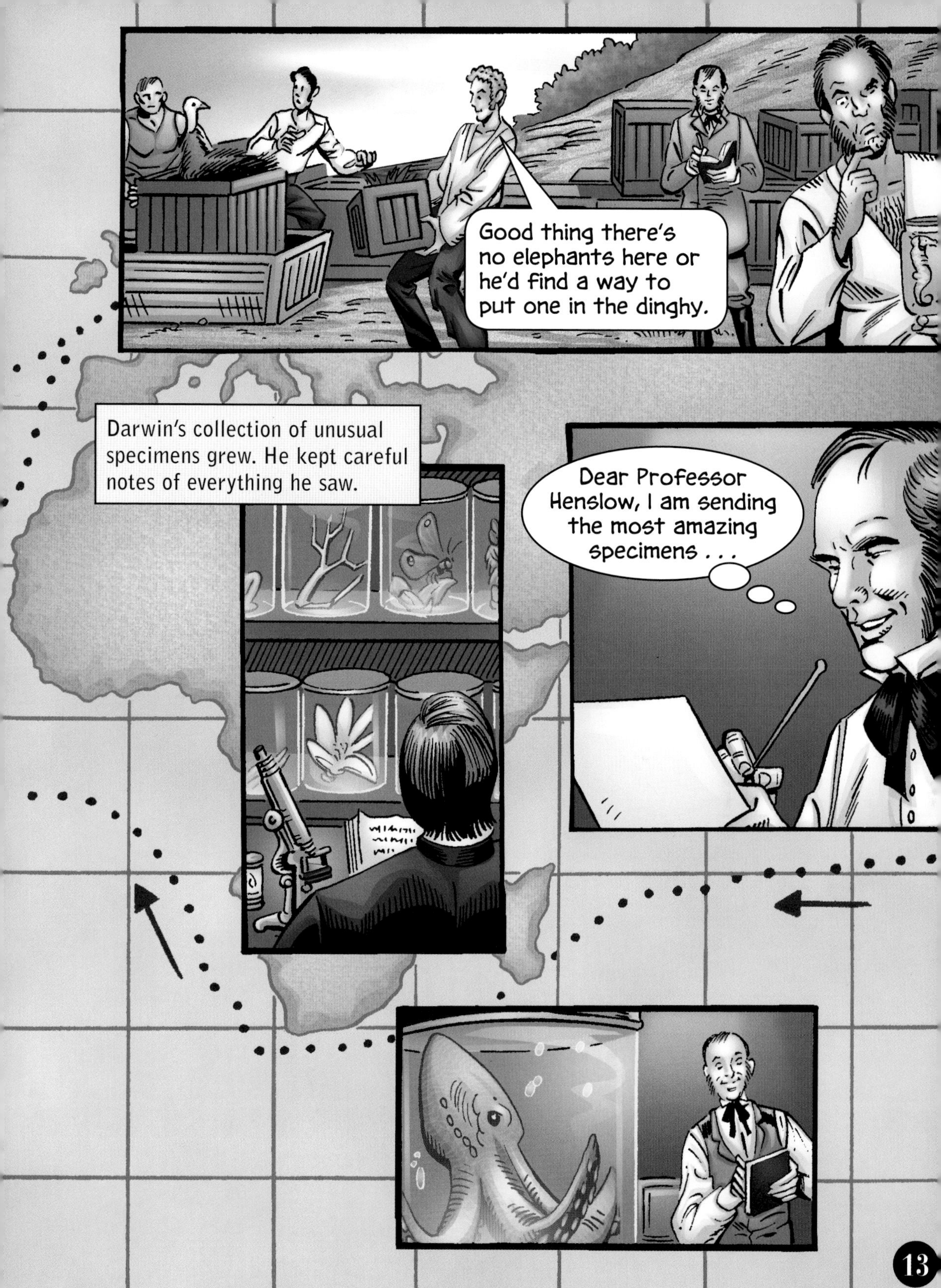
Good thing there's no elephants here or he'd find a way to put one in the dinghy.
Darwin's collection of unusual specimens grew. He kept careful notes of everything he saw.
Dear Professor Henslow, I am sending the most amazing specimens . . .

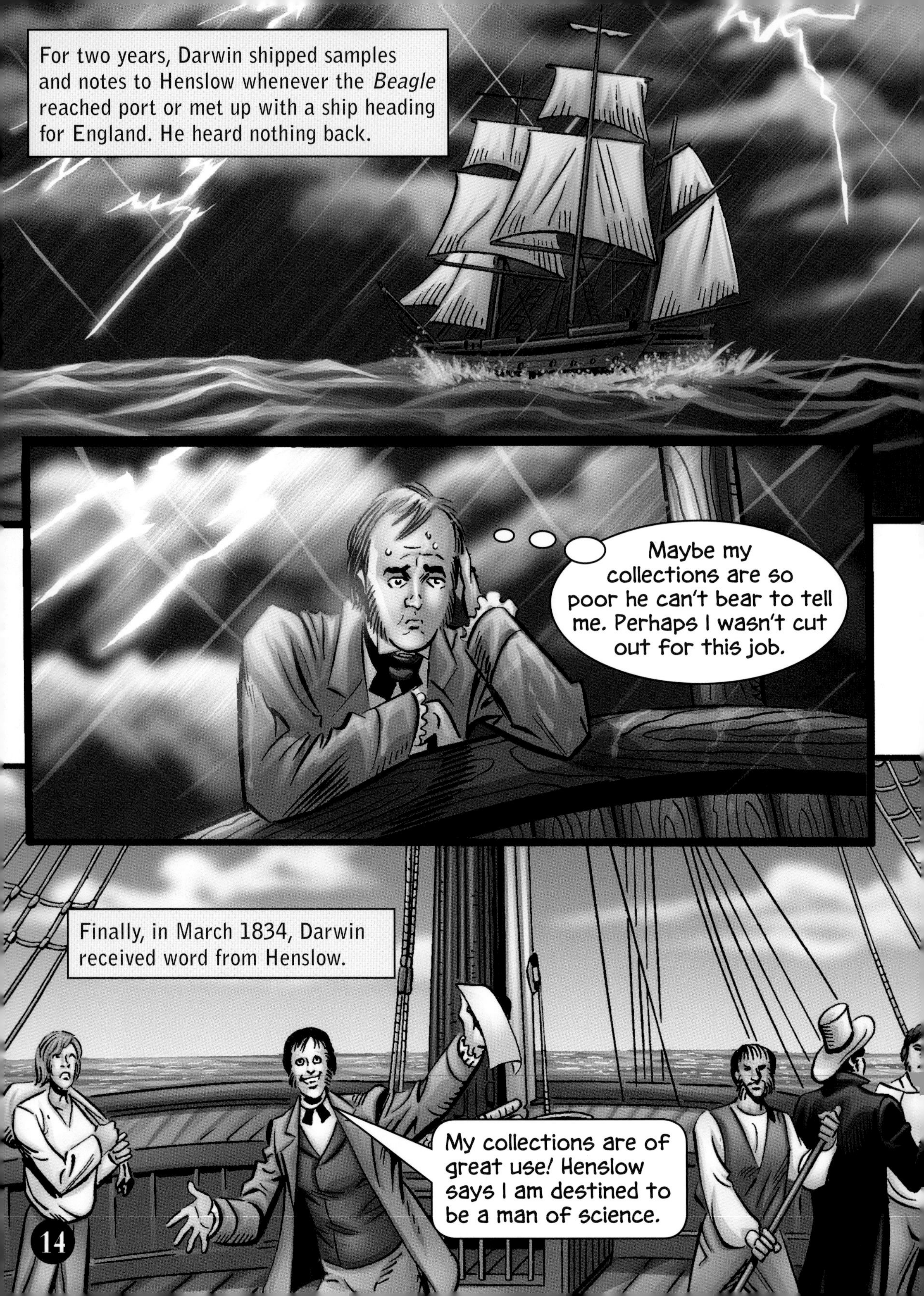
For two years, Darwin shipped samples and notes to Henslow whenever the *Beagle* reached port or met up with a ship heading for England. He heard nothing back.
Maybe my collections are so poor he can't bear to tell me. Perhaps I wasn't cut out for this job.
Finally, in March 1834, Darwin received word from Henslow.
My collections are of great use! Henslow says I am destined to be a man of science.

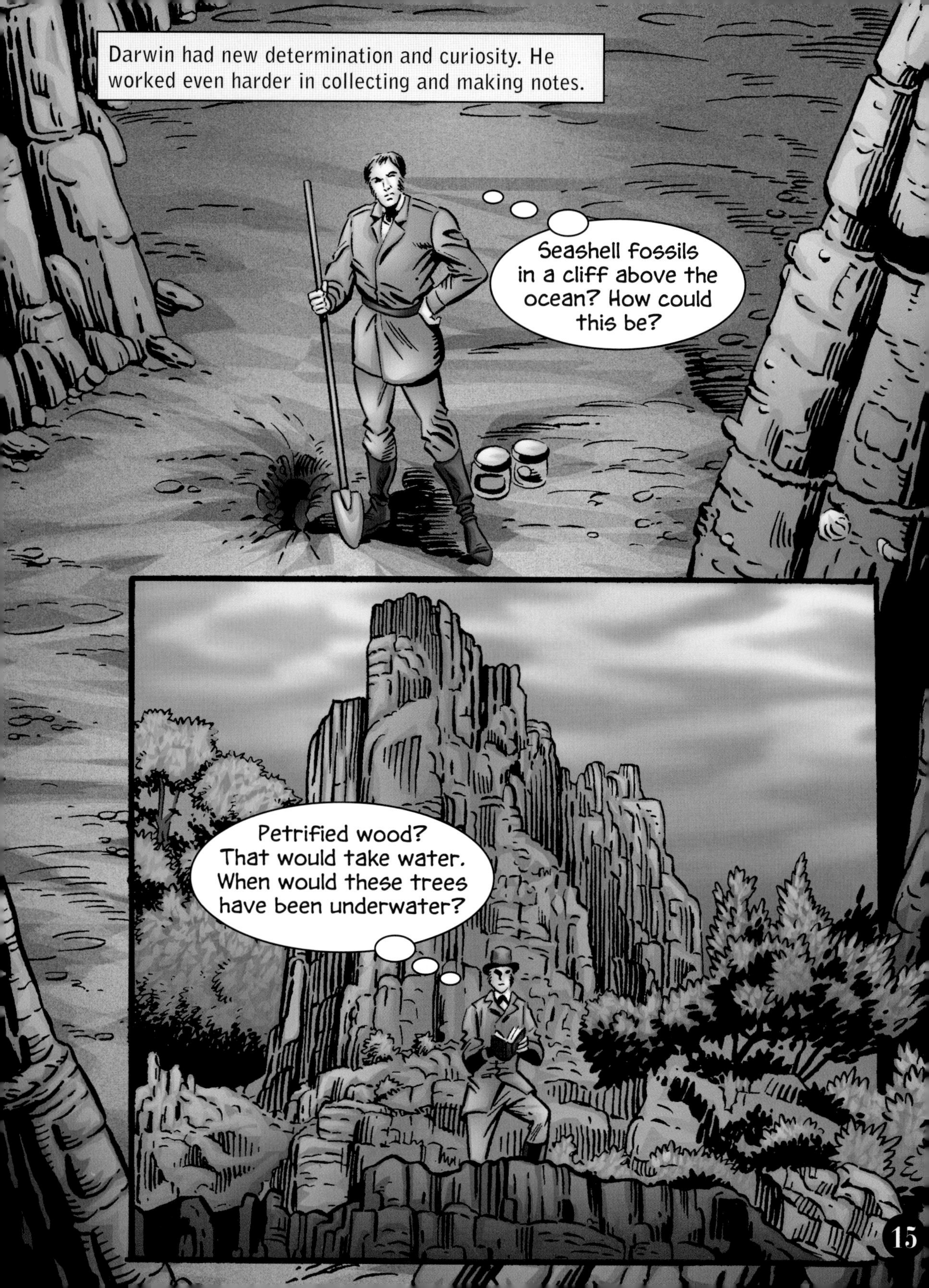
Darwin had new determination and curiosity. He worked even harder in collecting and making notes.
Seashell fossils in a cliff above the ocean? How could this be?
Petrified wood? That would take water. When would these trees have been underwater?

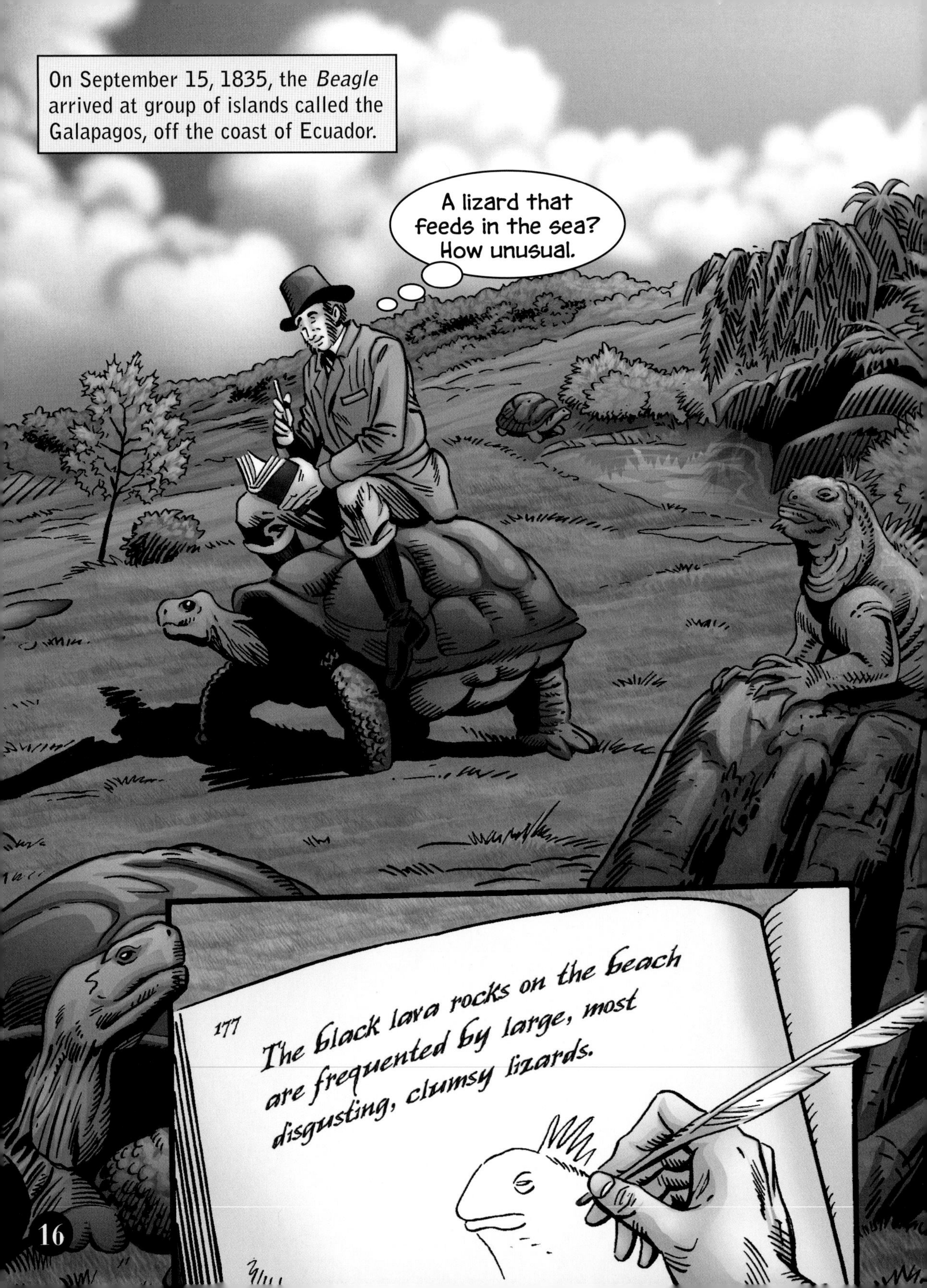
On September 15, 1835, the *Beagle* arrived at group of islands called the Galapagos, off the coast of Ecuador.
A lizard that feeds in the sea? How unusual.
177
The black lava rocks on the beach are frequented by large, most disgusting, clumsy lizards.

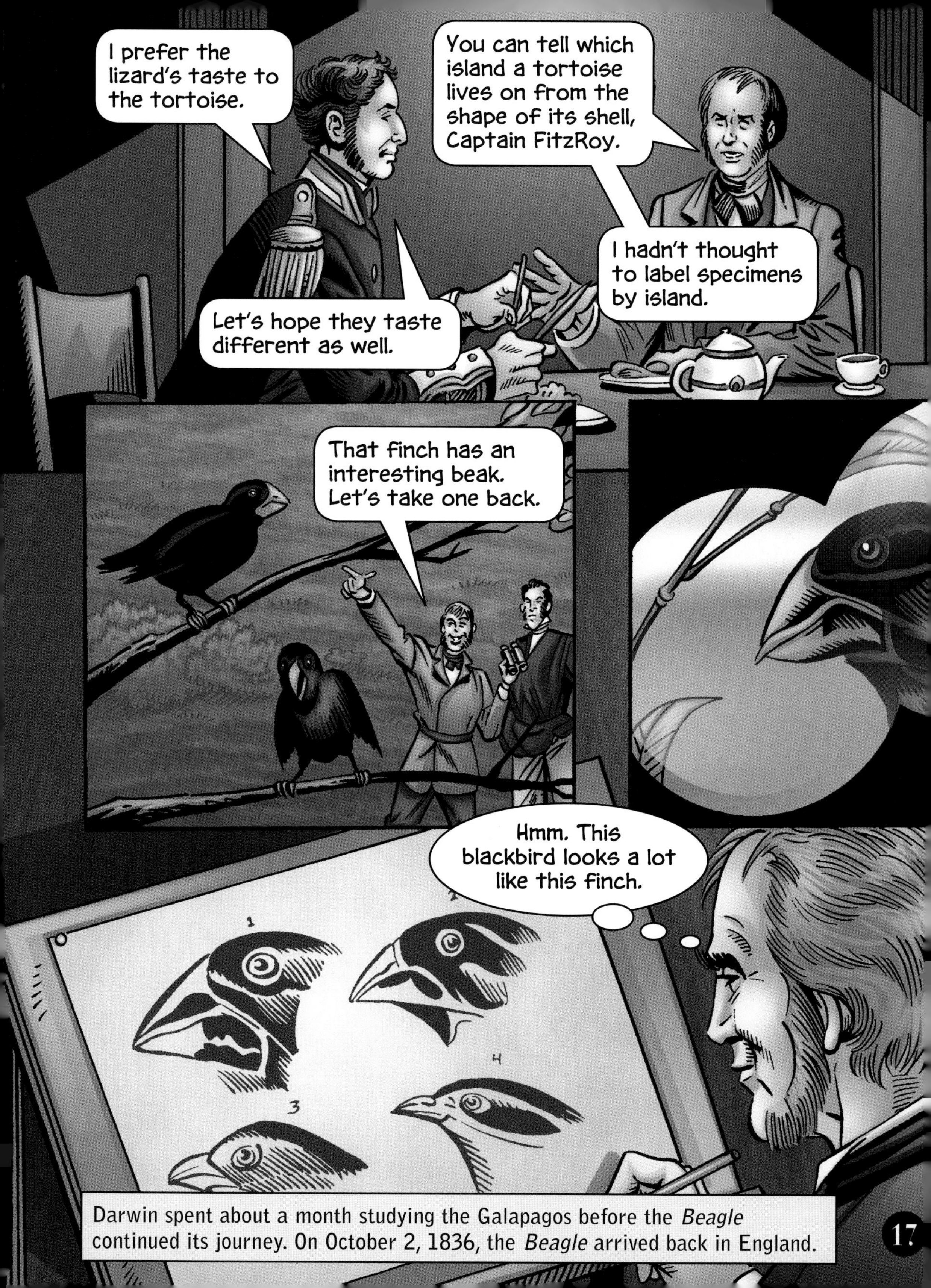
I prefer the lizard's taste to the tortoise.
You can tell which island a tortoise lives on from the shape of its shell, Captain FitzRoy.
Let's hope they taste different as well.
I hadn't thought to label specimens by island.
That finch has an interesting beak. Let's take one back.
Hmm. This blackbird looks a lot like this finch.
1
2
3
4

Darwin spent about a month studying the Galapagos before the *Beagle* continued its journey. On October 2, 1836, the *Beagle* arrived back in England.

CHAPTER 3
A THEORY COMES TOGETHER

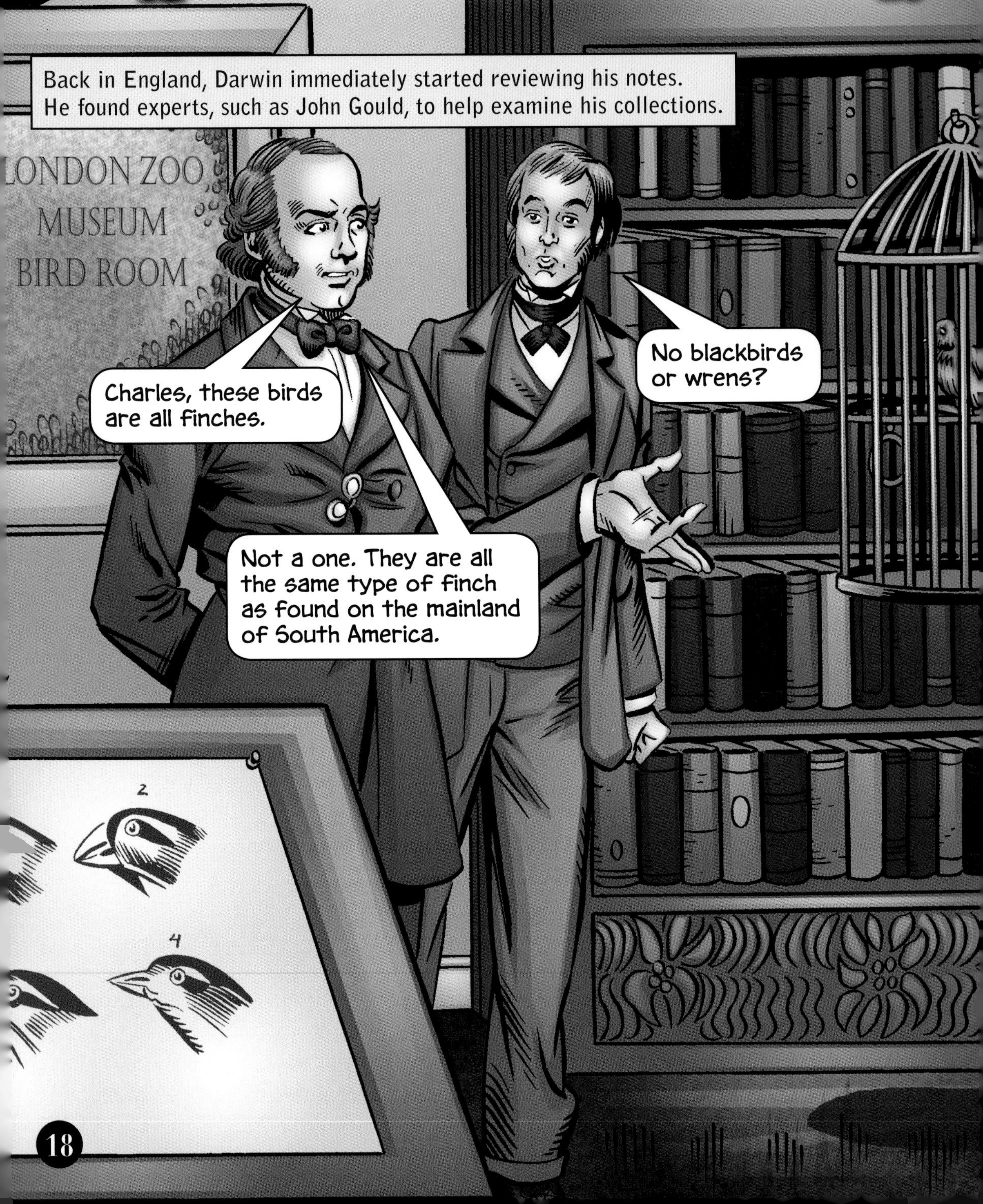
Back in England, Darwin immediately started reviewing his notes. He found experts, such as John Gould, to help examine his collections.
LONDON ZOO MUSEUM BIRD ROOM
Charles, these birds are all finches.
No blackbirds or wrens?
Not a one. They are all the same type of finch as found on the mainland of South America.
2
4

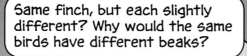

Same finch, but each slightly different? Why would the same birds have different beaks?

To eat different food. Small pointy beaks for bugs. Thick strong beaks for cracking open big seeds.

The birds seem to have changed along with the conditions of each island.

Were all these finches created differently from the beginning?

Or did one kind of finch actually adapt to the environment over time?

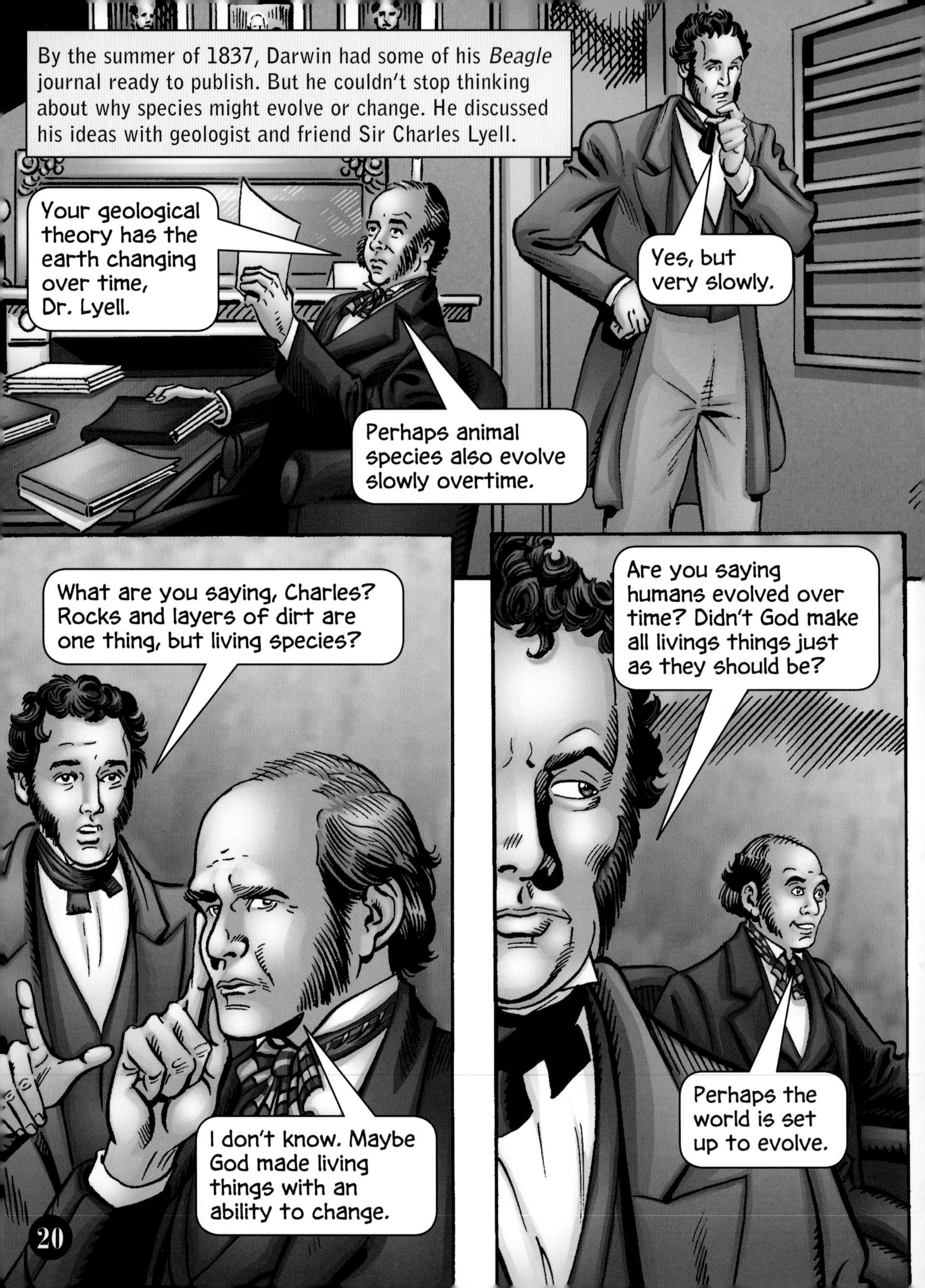
By the summer of 1837, Darwin had some of his *Beagle* journal ready to publish. But he couldn't stop thinking about why species might evolve or change. He discussed his ideas with geologist and friend Sir Charles Lyell.
Your geological theory has the earth changing over time, Dr. Lyell.
Yes, but very slowly.
Perhaps animal species also evolve slowly overtime.
What are you saying, Charles? Rocks and layers of dirt are one thing, but living species?
I don't know. Maybe God made living things with an ability to change.
Are you saying humans evolved over time? Didn't God make all livings things just as they should be?
Perhaps the world is set up to evolve.

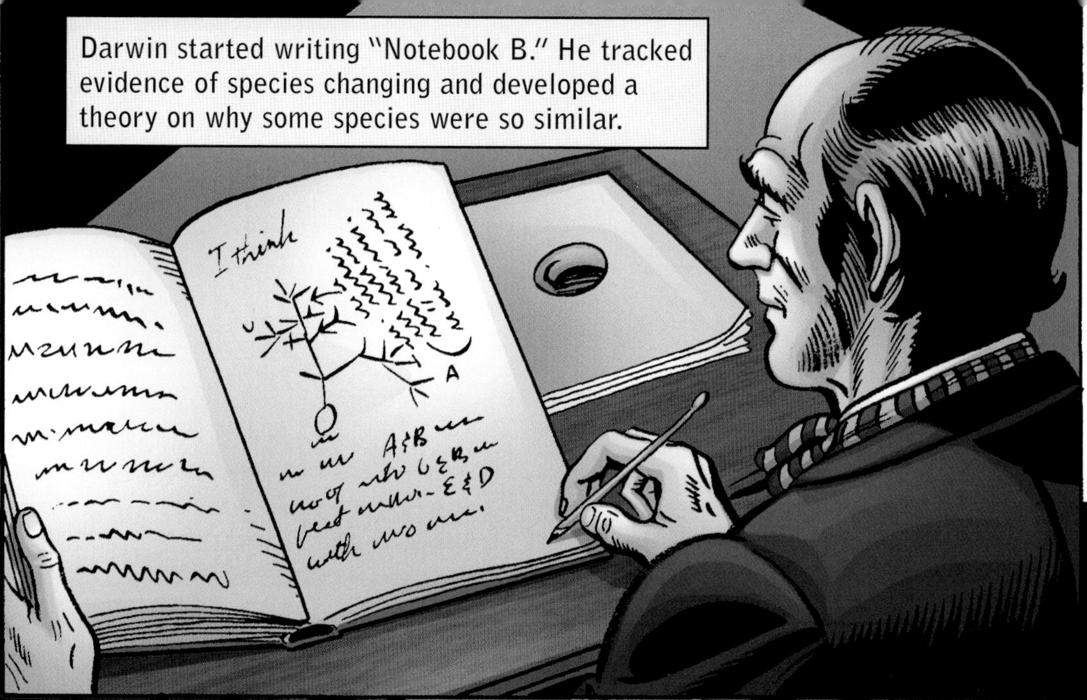
Darwin started writing "Notebook B." He tracked evidence of species changing and developed a theory on why some species were so similar.
I think
A

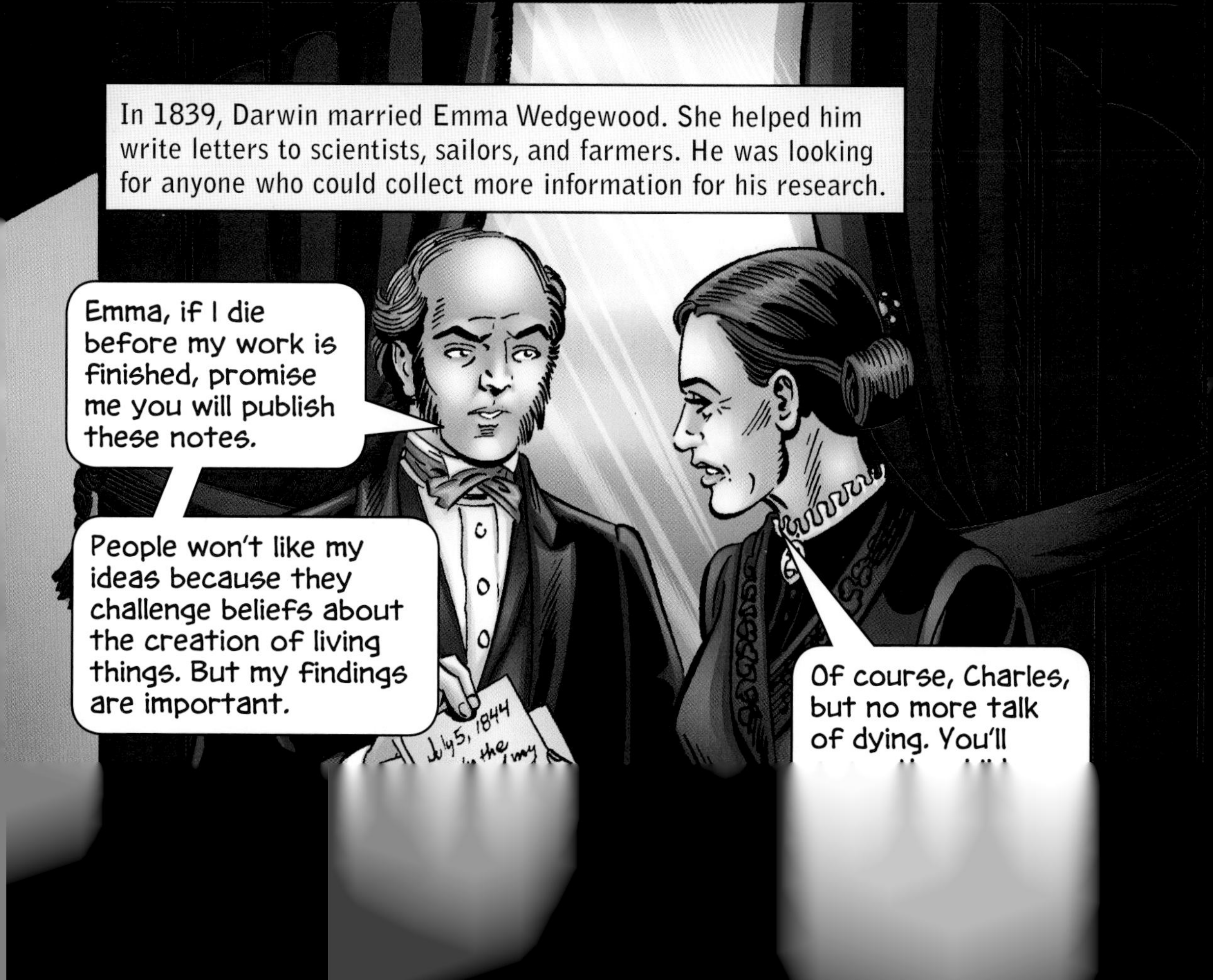
In 1839, Darwin married Emma Wedgewood. She helped him write letters to scientists, sailors, and farmers. He was looking for anyone who could collect more information for his research.
Emma, if I die before my work is finished, promise me you will publish these notes.
People won't like my ideas because they challenge beliefs about the creation of living things. But my findings are important.
Of course, Charles, but no more talk of dying. You'll
July 5, 1844

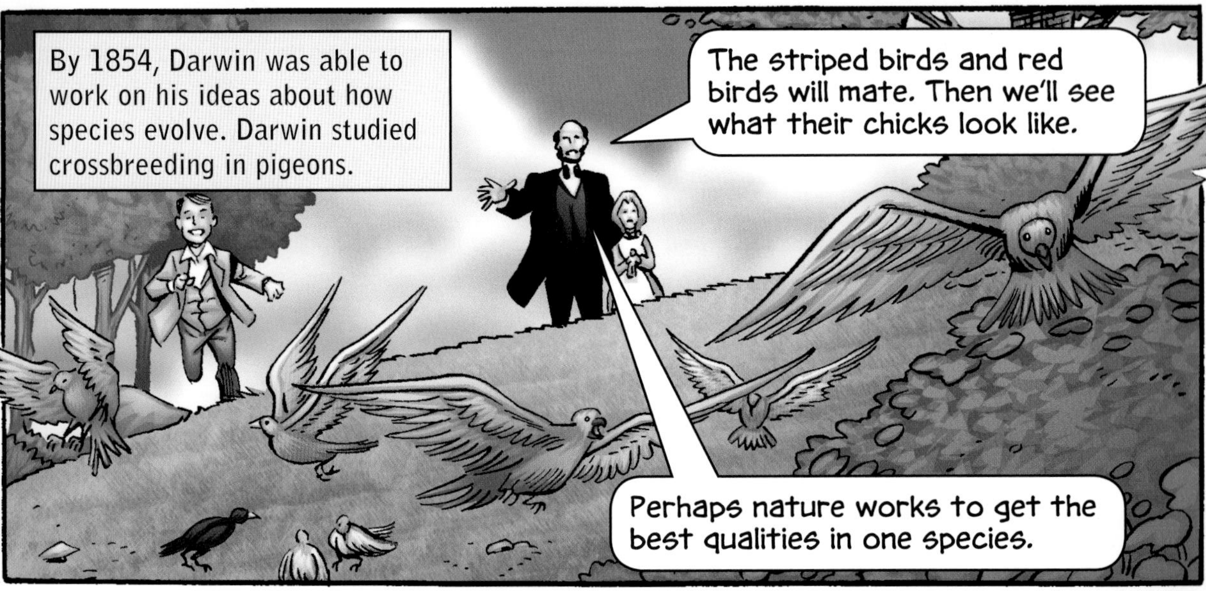
By 1854, Darwin was able to work on his ideas about how species evolve. Darwin studied crossbreeding in pigeons.
The striped birds and red birds will mate. Then we'll see what their chicks look like.
Perhaps nature works to get the best qualities in one species.

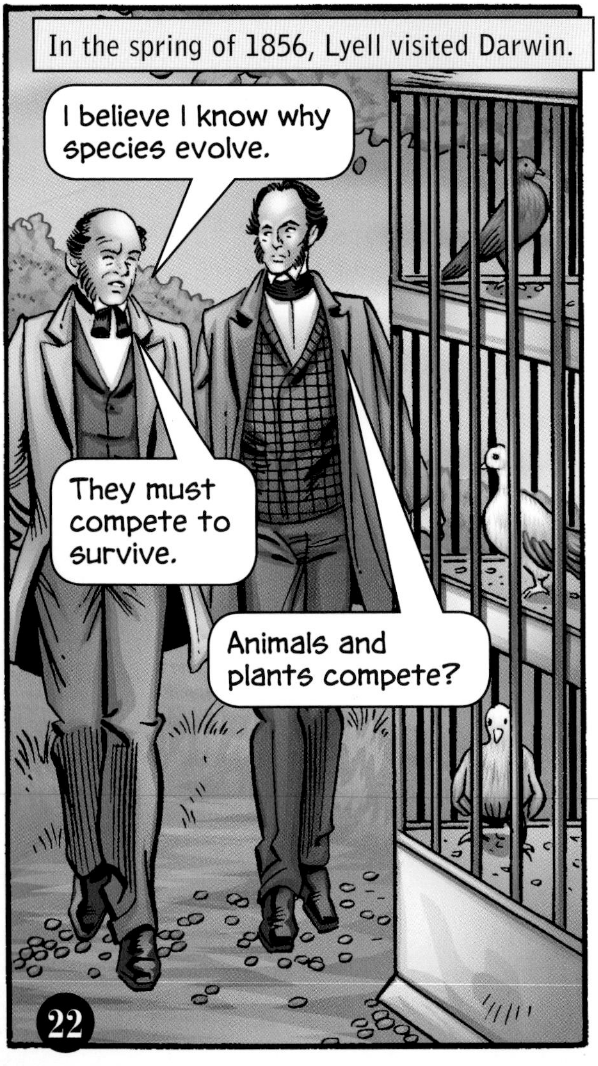
In the spring of 1856, Lyell visited Darwin.
I believe I know why species evolve.
They must compete to survive.
Animals and plants compete?

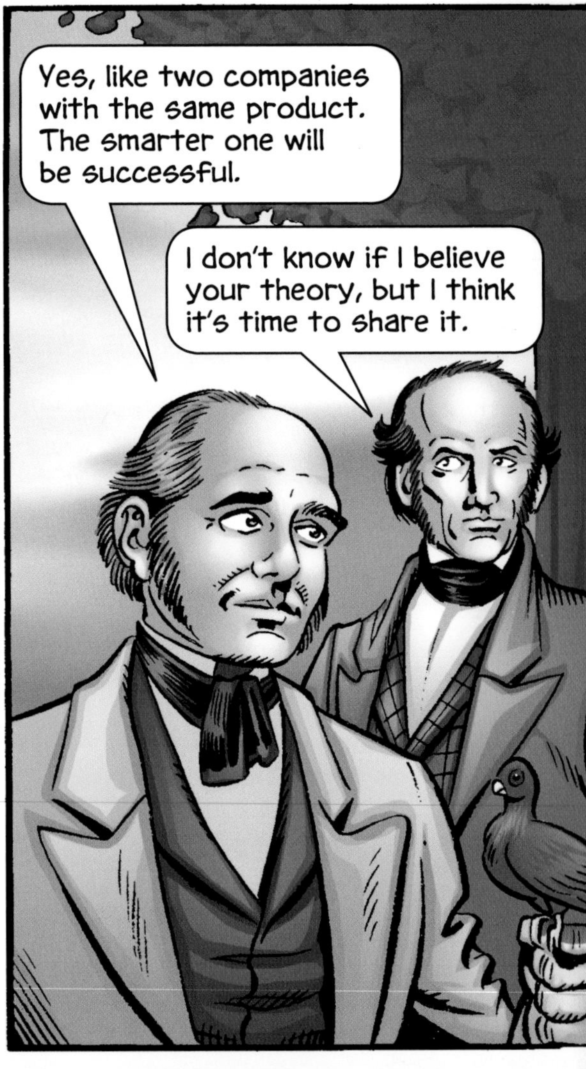
Yes, like two companies with the same product. The smarter one will be successful.
I don't know if I believe your theory, but I think it's time to share it.

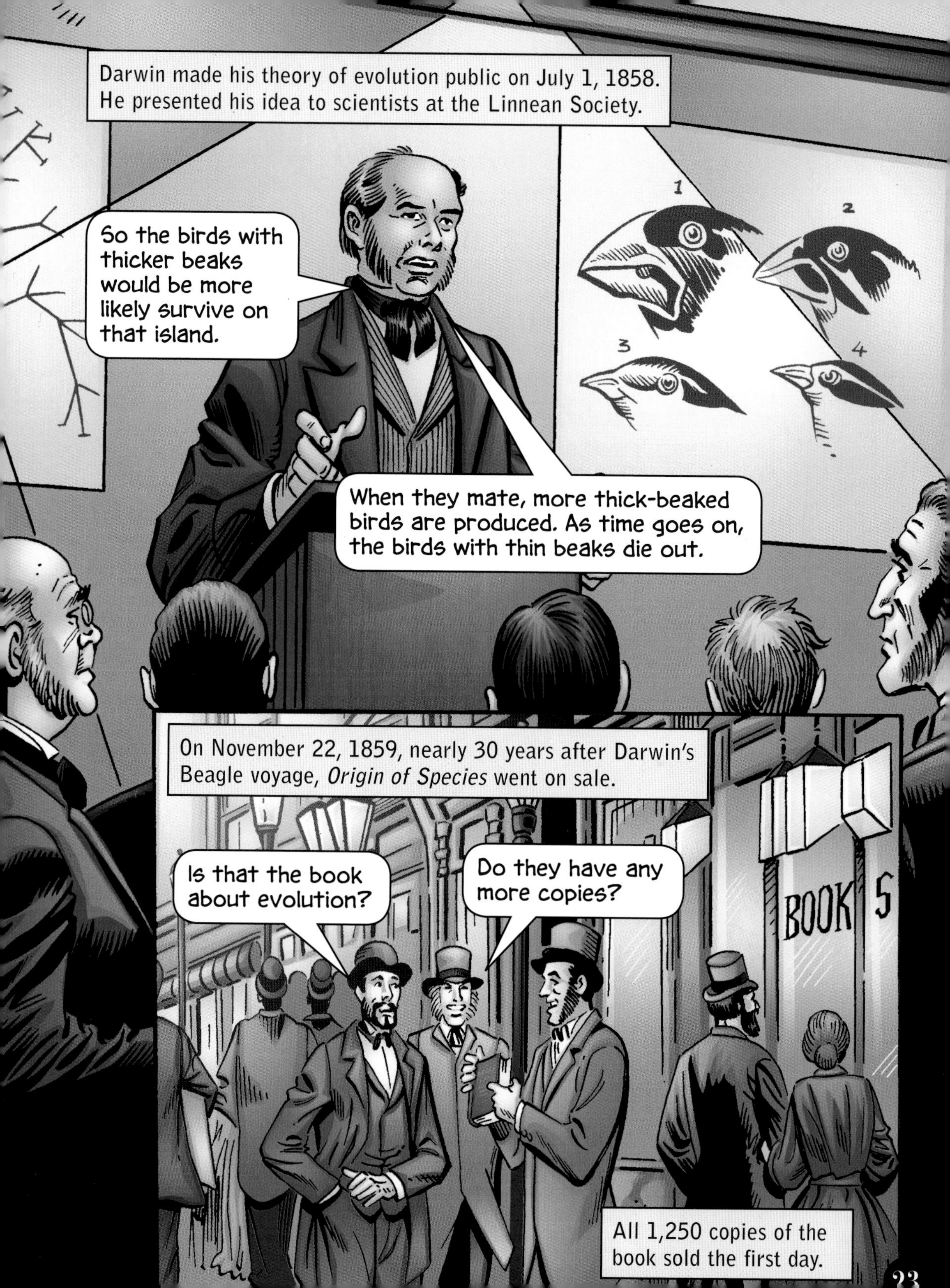

Darwin made his theory of evolution public on July 1, 1858. He presented his idea to scientists at the Linnean Society.
So the birds with thicker beaks would be more likely survive on that island.
1
2
3
4
When they mate, more thick-beaked birds are produced. As time goes on, the birds with thin beaks die out.
On November 22, 1859, nearly 30 years after Darwin's Beagle voyage, *Origin of Species* went on sale.
Is that the book about evolution?
Do they have any more copies?
BOOKS
All 1,250 copies of the book sold the first day.

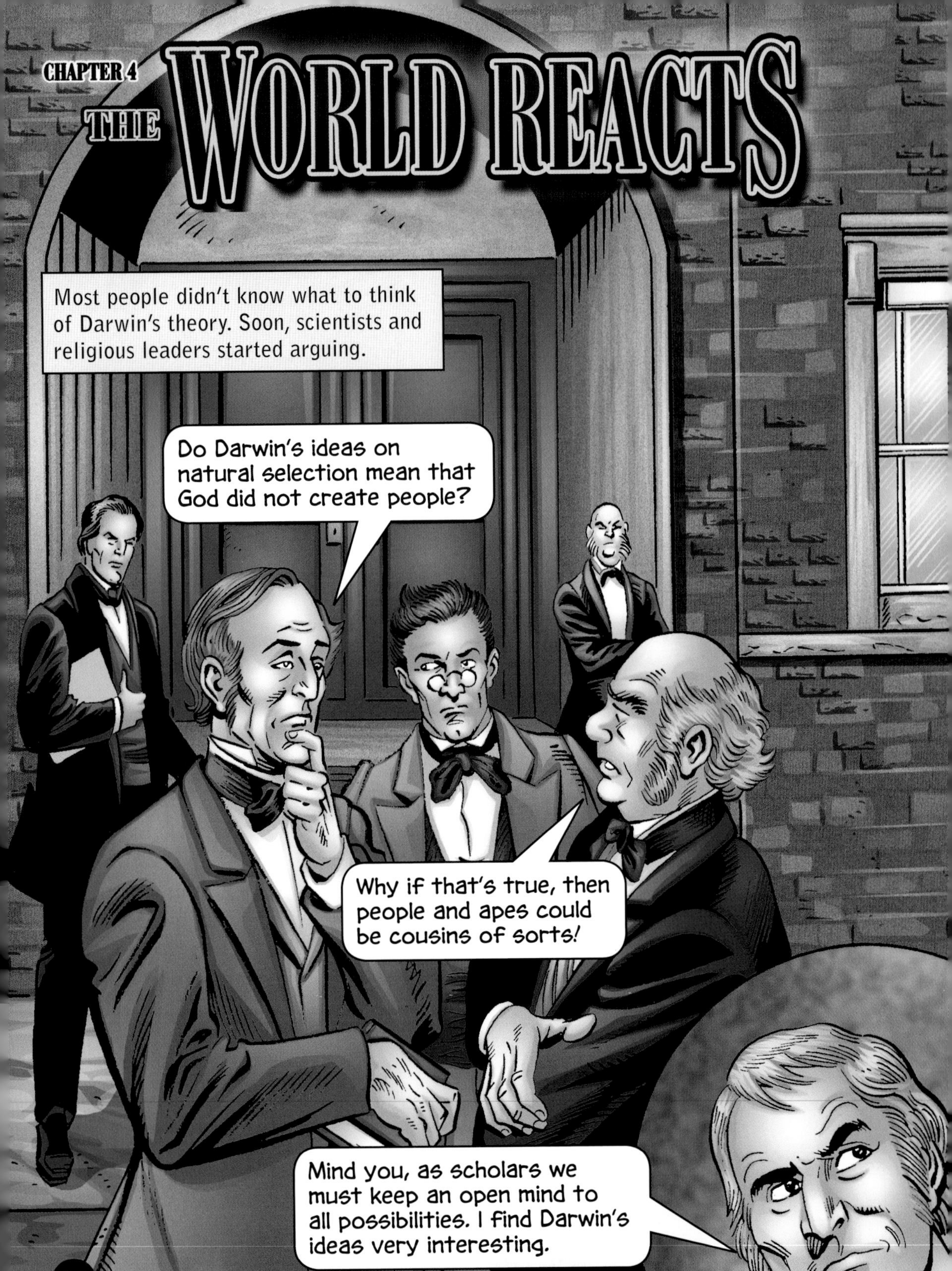
CHAPTER 4
THE WORLD REACTS
Most people didn't know what to think of Darwin's theory. Soon, scientists and religious leaders started arguing.
Do Darwin's ideas on natural selection mean that God did not create people?
Why if that's true, then people and apes could be cousins of sorts!
Mind you, as scholars we must keep an open mind to all possibilities. I find Darwin's ideas very interesting.

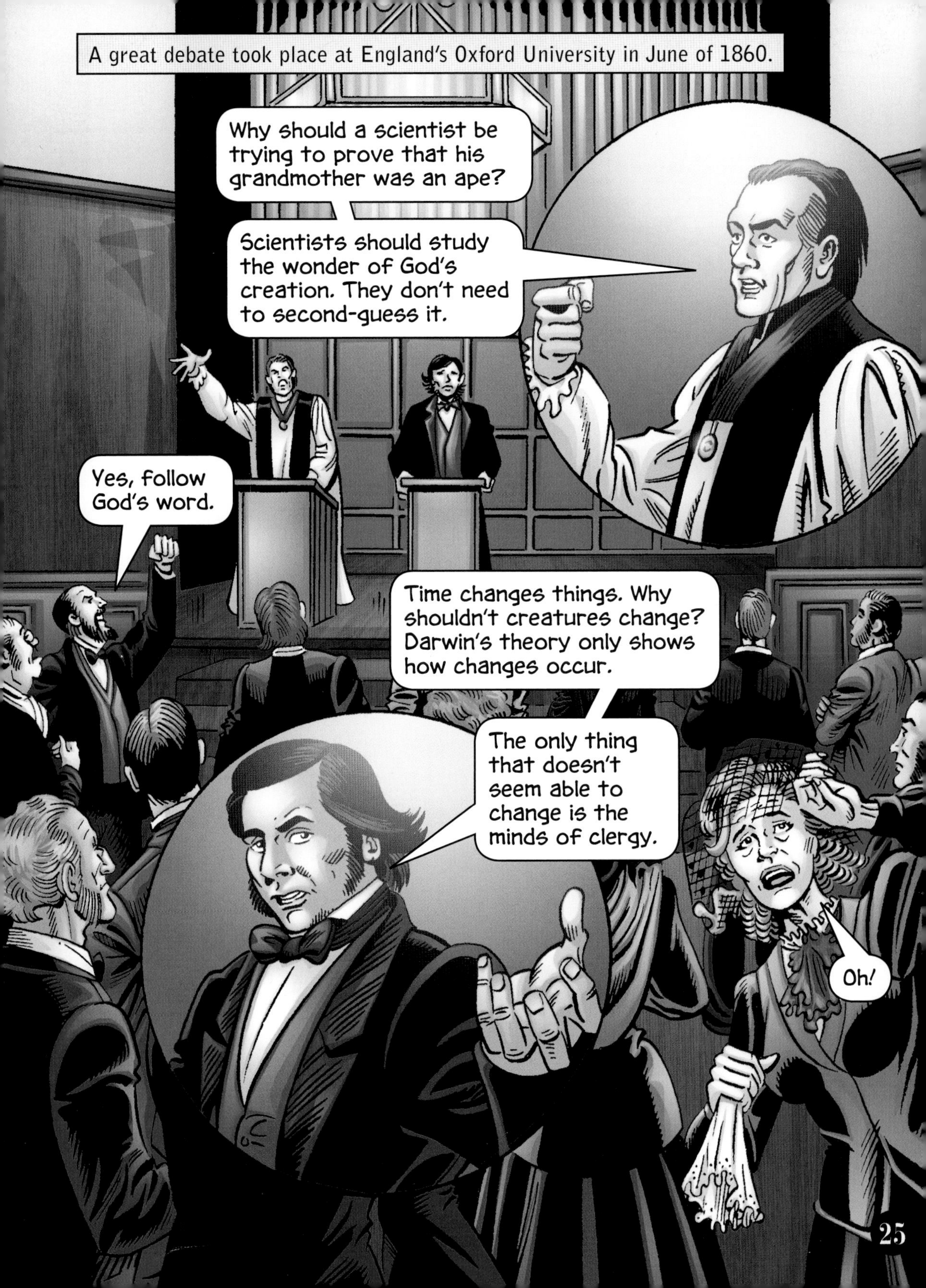
A great debate took place at England's Oxford University in June of 1860.
Why should a scientist be trying to prove that his grandmother was an ape?
Scientists should study the wonder of God's creation. They don't need to second-guess it.
Yes, follow God's word.
Time changes things. Why shouldn't creatures change? Darwin's theory only shows how changes occur.
The only thing that doesn't seem able to change is the minds of clergy.
Oh!

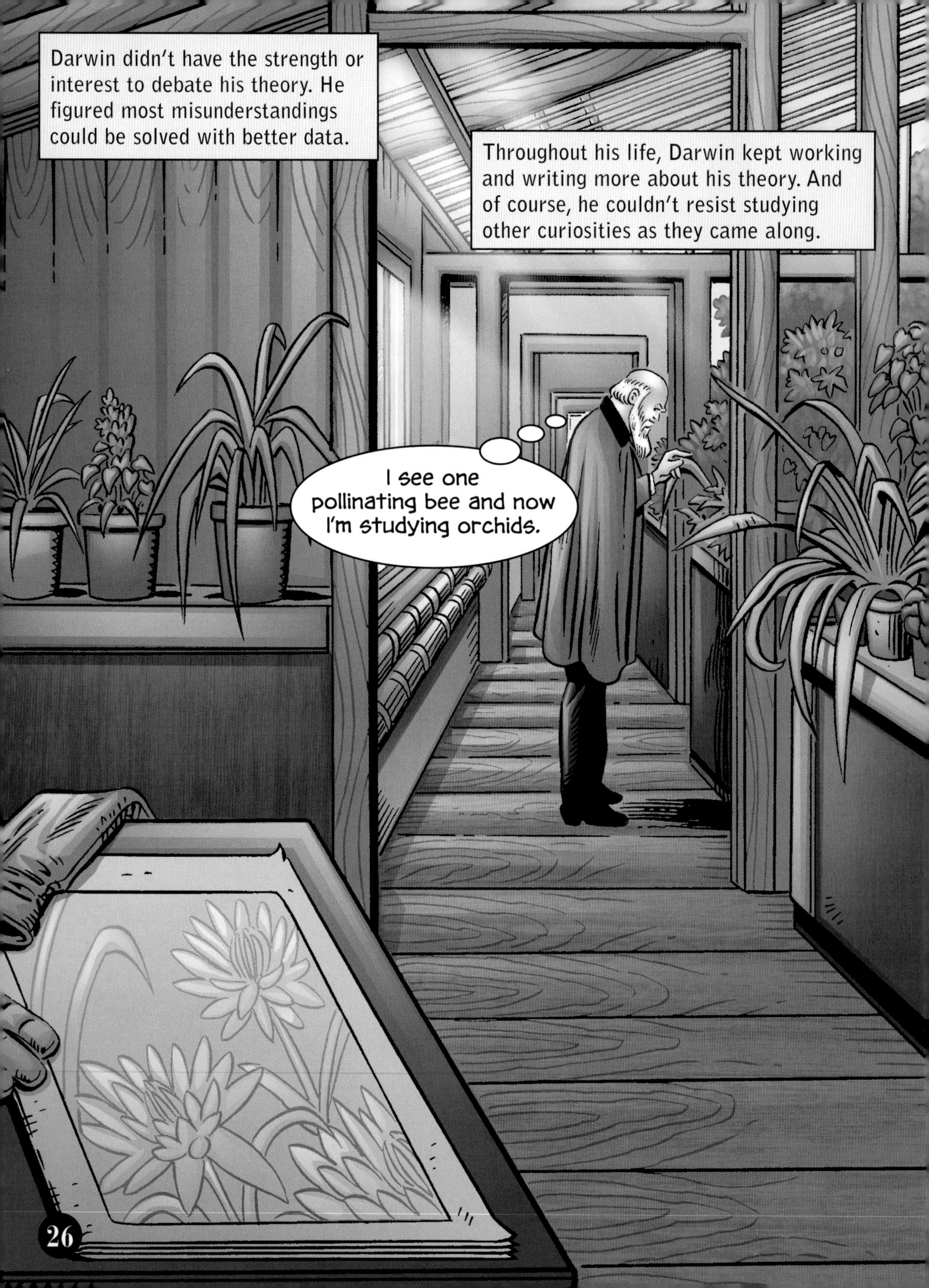
Darwin didn't have the strength or interest to debate his theory. He figured most misunderstandings could be solved with better data.
Throughout his life, Darwin kept working and writing more about his theory. And of course, he couldn't resist studying other curiosities as they came along.
I see one pollinating bee and now I'm studying orchids.

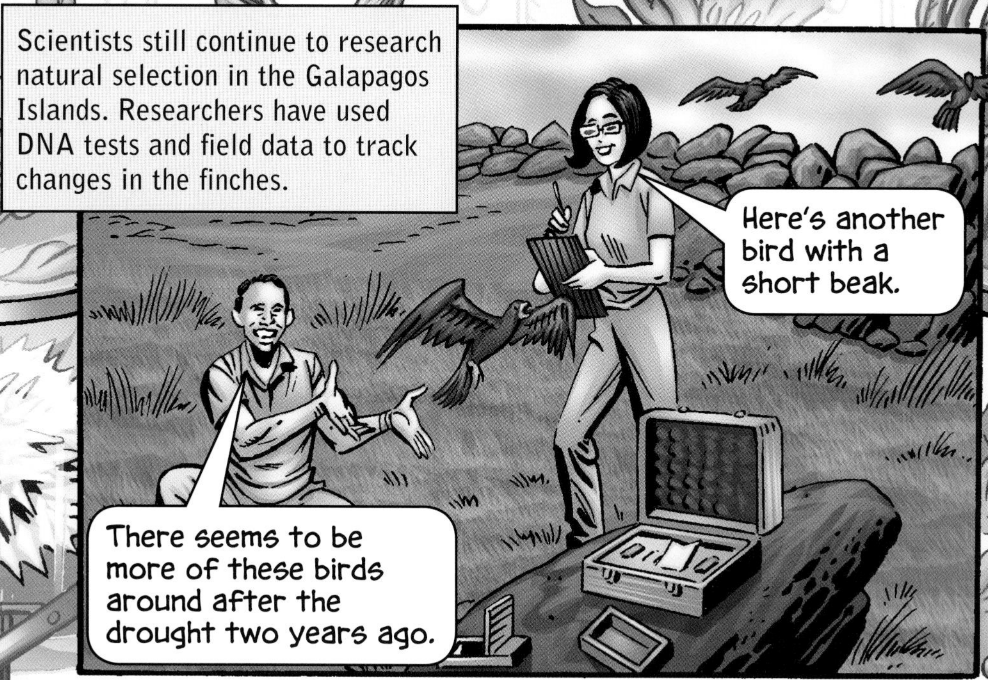
Scientists still continue to research natural selection in the Galapagos Islands. Researchers have used DNA tests and field data to track changes in the finches.
Here's another bird with a short beak.
There seems to be more of these birds around after the drought two years ago.

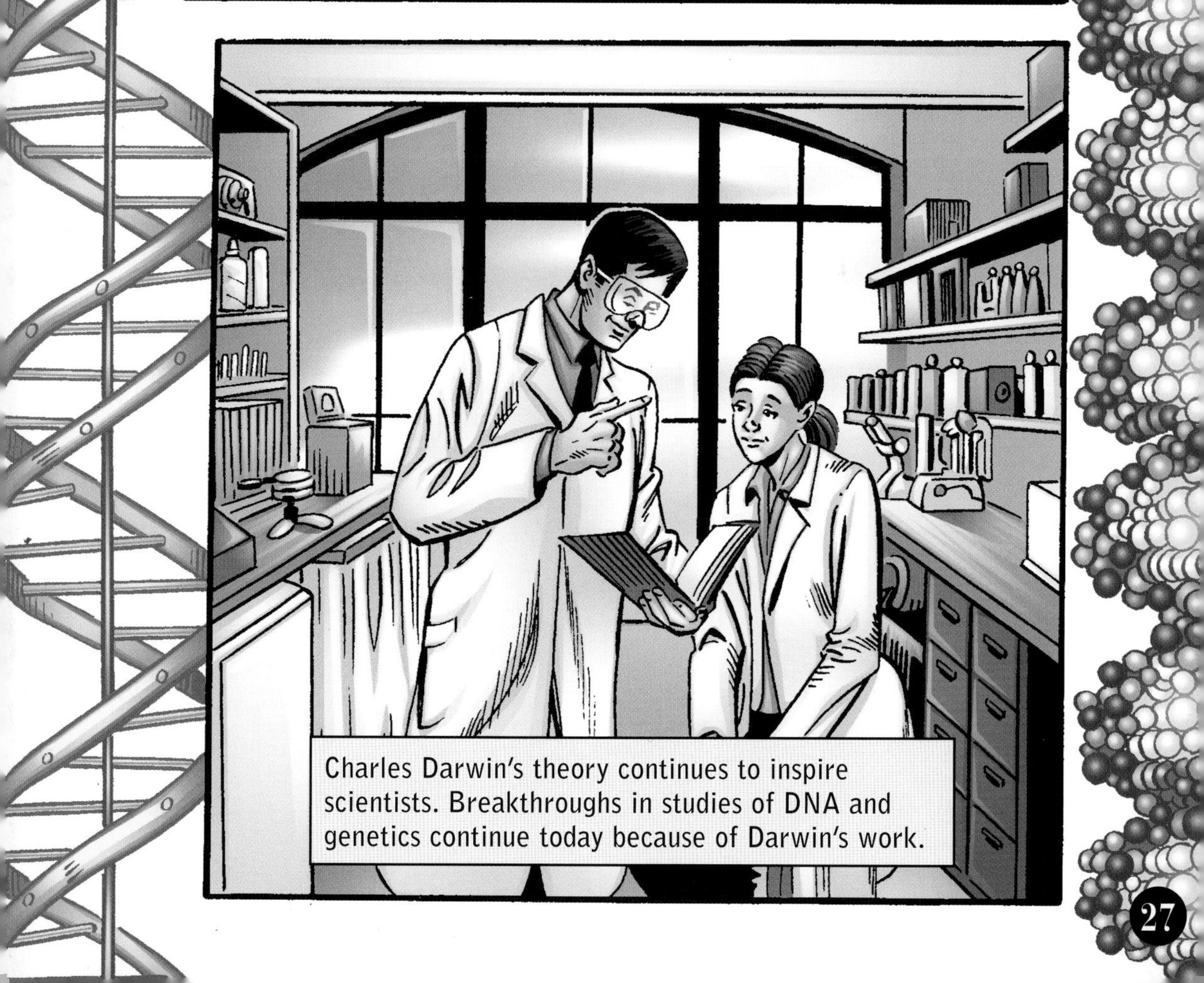
Charles Darwin's theory continues to inspire scientists. Breakthroughs in studies of DNA and genetics continue today because of Darwin's work.

MORE ABOUT DARWIN
AND EVOLUTION

 Charles Darwin was born February 12, 1809, in Shrewsbury, England. Darwin struggled with illness for years after his *Beagle* voyage. He died April 19, 1882, at his home in Kent, England.

 Ideas of evolution have been around for centuries. Even early Greek myths had ideas about species changing. Darwin's theory of natural selection was different because it addressed how and why species evolved.

 Darwin started Notebook B in July 1837. By November 1838, Darwin's ideas and questions had expanded into Notebooks C, D, E, M, and N.

 A 1925 court case, *Scopes versus State*, sparked a debate about Darwin and the teaching of evolution. The case became known as the Scopes Monkey Trial. Reporters from around the world covered the case.

 Darwin was known as an unusual father. Most wealthy Englishmen did not spend much time with their children. Instead, they paid workers to care for them. But Darwin played with his kids. He took them for walks and let them help in his lab. He was their favorite playmate.

Darwin first grew his famous beard in 1866. Some say he grew it so people wouldn't recognize him in public.

Darwin was often sick in bed and he passed the time writing letters. More than 15,000 letters to and from Darwin have been collected by Cambridge University in England.

While traveling in South America, Darwin was often bitten by assassin bugs. These blood-sucking beetles can carry Chagas' disease. Darwin describes being attacked by the bugs: "It is most disgusting to feel soft wingless insects, about an inch long, crawling over one's body. Before sucking they are quite thin, but afterward they become round and bloated with blood, and in this state are easily crushed."

In honor of his curiosity and research, Darwin has had many things named after him including the Galapagos finches, an ostrich-like bird called a rhea, a mountain, and even a European space mission.

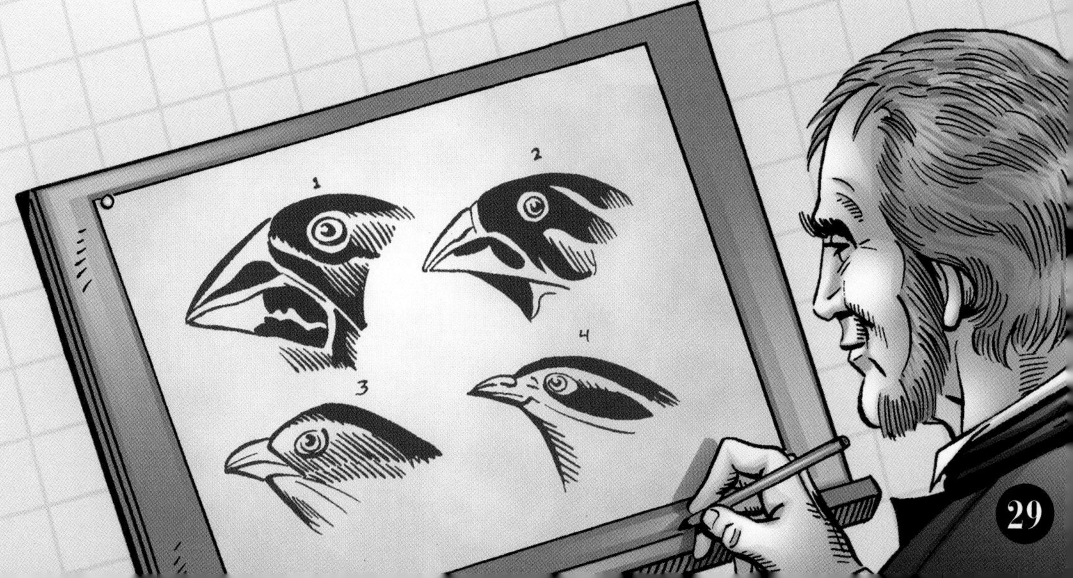
1
2
3
4

GLOSSARY

adapt (uh-DAPT)—to change to fit into a different or new environment

crossbreed (KROSS-breed)—to cross two varieties or breeds of the same species by mating

DNA (dee-en-AYE)—material in cells that gives people, plants, and animals their individual characteristics

evolve (e-VOLV)—when something develops over a long time with gradual changes

petrified wood (PET-ruh-fide WOOD)—wood that has been changed into a stony substance by water and minerals

species (SPEE-sheez)—a group of plants or animals that share common characteristics

specimen (SPESS-uh-muhn)—a sample or example used to stand for a whole group

INTERNET SITES

FactHound offers a safe, fun way to find Internet sites related to this book. All of the sites on FactHound have been researched by our staff.

Here's how:
1. Visit *www.facthound.com*
2. Choose your grade level.
3. Type in this book ID **1429601450** for age-appropriate sites. You may also browse subjects by clicking on letters, or by clicking on pictures and words.
4. Click on the **Fetch It** button.

FactHound will fetch the best sites for you!

READ MORE

Anderson, Margaret Jean. *Charles Darwin: Naturalist.* Great Minds of Science. Berkeley Heights, N.J.: Enslow, 2007.

Fleisher, Paul. *Evolution.* Great Ideas of Science. Minneapolis: Lerner, 2006.

Macdonald, Fiona. *Inside the Beagle with Charles Darwin.* New York: Enchanted Lion Books, 2005.

Sìs, Peter. *The Tree of Life: A Book Depicting the Life of Charles Darwin, Naturalist, Geologist, and Thinker.* New York: Farrar Straus Giroux, 2003.

BIBLIOGRAPHY

Darwin, Charles. *On the Origin of Species by Means of Natural Selection, or The Preservation of Favored Races in the Struggle for Life.* New York: D. Appleton and Company, 1881.

Darwin, Francis, editor. *The Autobiography of Charles Darwin.* Great Minds Series. Amherst, N.Y. : Prometheus Books, 2000.

Darwin, Francis. *The Life and Letters of Charles Darwin.* New York: D. Appleton & Co., 1901.

INDEX